IP.

10TH GENERATION

USER GUIDE

The Complete Manual for Beginners and Seniors to Set up and Master the Latest Apple iPad With Tips And Tricks For iPadOS 17

BY

JOHNSON SMITH

Copyright © 2024 Johnson Smith

TABLE OF CONTENTS

CHAPTER ONE

SETUP FUNDAMENTALS

iPad has a straightforward configuration procedure that will assist you in getting started as soon as you power on the device. You've arrived at the proper place, whether you're just getting begun or simply want to verify that the fundamentals are in place.

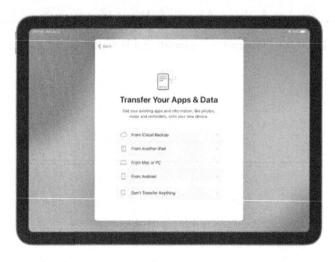

Transferring apps and information via the iCloud backup, a different iPad, a PC or Mac, and an Android device is an option on the configuration interface.

TRANSFER INFORMATION AND APPLICATIONS TO YOUR NEW IPAD

Many of the apps, settings, and data from the previous iPad can be transferred wirelessly to your new iPad when you first power it on and start the setup process; simply bring both devices together and follow the on-screen instructions.

Wi-Fi is selected in the Settings sidebar located on the left edge of the display. On the right edge of the display, the network is selected and Wi-Fi is enabled.

ESTABLISH WI-FI CONNECTIVITY AND CELLULAR SERVICE

Select your household Wi-Fi network from the Settings ⚙ > Wi-Fi menu to attach your iPad to it. iPad establishes an internet connection automatically whenever you are at home.

Using an eSIM, you can enable cellular service on the iPad if you are using the Wi-Fi + Cellular model (access Settings ⚙ > Cellular Data). Install an alternative nano-SIM supplied by your carrier.

The Settings interface, featuring the Apple Identification
sign-in dialogue situated centrally

ENTERING YOUR APPLE ID TO LOG IN

You use your Apple ID to access iCloud, iMessage,
Apple Music, FaceTime, and a variety of other services.
You may create an Apple ID if you do not already have
one.

To sign in to the device using your Apple ID, navigate to
Settings ⊚ > Sign in. If you possess an iPadOS 17 or
newer and an iPhone (running iOS 17 and later). or
another iPad, you can easily position your iPad near the
other device. You may sign in manually if not. Navigate
to Settings ⊚ > [your name] to ensure that you are
signed in; your Apple ID will be displayed below your
name.

On the left edge of the display, in the Settings sidebar, Touch ID and Passcode are selected. Touch ID feature unlock options are located on the right edge of the screen. Password Autofill, iPad Unlock, Wallet and Apple Pay, and iTunes & App Store are all deactivated.

CONFIGURE TOUCH ID OR FACE ID

Face ID (face detection) or Touch ID (fingerprint) can be employed to authenticate users of an iPad, conduct purchases, and unlock applications securely. Touch ID and Face ID information remains on your device as well as is not stored elsewhere for your protection.

Perform one of the subsequent actions, counting down from your iPad model:

❖ Face ID configuration: Navigate to Settings ⚙️ > Face ID and Passcode, select Face ID configuration, and then adhere to the on-screen prompts.

❖ Navigate to Settings ⚙️ > Touch ID and Passcode, select Add a Fingerprint, and then adhere to the instructions displayed on-screen.

11

The user's name is selected from the Settings sidebar located at the top of the display on the left. There are options on the right edge of the display for selecting which Find My functions to activate. Sharing My Location and Find My iPad are both enabled.

ENABLE FIND MY IPAD

iPads are trackable if they are lost or stolen.

Press Find My iPad in the Settings > [your username] > Find My section, then toggle Find My iPad on.

The location of the gadgets is visible through the Find My app. If you misplace your iPad and have no access to the Find My application, you can use Find Deviceson iCloud.com to locate your device.

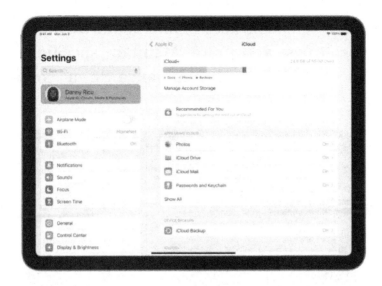

The Settings interface, featuring the user's name is highlighted in the sidebar located at the left-hand corner of the display. Options for iCloud settings, which include the storage capacity meter and a list of applications and features (including pictures, iCloud Drive, iCloud Mail, as well as Passwords and Keychain), are located on the right edge of the screen

YOUR DATA IS STORED IN ICLOUD

iCloud enables you to synchronize and safeguard sensitive data across all of your devices. If you replace, misplace, damage, or theft your iPad, your iCloud-stored pictures, videos, backups, and other data will remain secure.

To enable or modify the desired iCloud features, navigate to Settings > [your username] > iCloud.

PERSONALIZE THE IPAD

The iPad can be customized to suit an individual's taste and interests. Customize the Lock Screen as well as the

Home Screen, enable accessibility features, modify your privacy settings, and more. Maintain specific features such as text size and luminance in a convenient location.

The iPad security screen is occupied by an image of the Earth. Widgets for the time, calendar, signals, weather, as well as the pencil's battery, are located on the left side.

CUSTOMIZE THE LOCK SCREEN

It is possible to display a preferred image, incorporate features and filters, and modify the font size of the time and date.

Press and hold the security screen, then select the Add New icon located at the bottom of the display, to begin. Tap one of the available options from the gallery to modify its appearance. Once you have designed a satisfactory Lock Screen, select Add followed by Set as Background Pair.

The iPad's home interface. Customized icons for the following applications are located at the top of the display: Clock, Locate My, Weather, pictures, and Calendar.

IMPLEMENT ELEMENTS IN THE HOME SCREEN

Widgets facilitate quick access to critical information, such as current weather conditions and forthcoming calendar events.

Tap and hold the picture you want to use on any display page until the applications begin to vibrate, and then select the Add Widget icon. Choose a widget, then select Add Widget after swiping to the right or left to observe the available sizes.

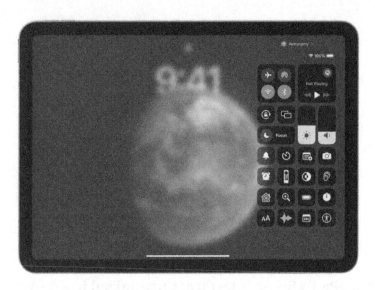

IPad users can personalize the Control Centre by adding functions like a timer, stopwatch, as well as voice memos.

CONFIGURE PREFERRED CONTROLS

Certain iPad functions—such as the timer and silent mode—can be accessed with a swipe in the Control Centre. To access the Control Centre rapidly, use the directional sweep from the upper-right corner.

Additional controls, such as text size and alarm, can be added to the Control Centre. To rearrange or remove controls, navigate to Settings ⚙ > Control Centre.

The Settings menu for the iPad. Accessibility is selected in the Settings sidebar located on the far left side of the screen. The option to modify accessibility features is located on the right edge of the display.

UTILIZE INTEGRATED ACCESSIBILITY FEATURES

Numerous accessibility features on the iPad accommodate your hearing, vision, sensory, motor, and educational requirements. Customize the appearance of text, enable subtitles and captioning, facilitate touchscreen operation, and more.

To modify these options, navigate to the Settings > Accessibility menu.

The Settings menu for the iPad. The Privacy & Security option is located in the Settings sidebar on the left edge of the screen. There is an option on the right edge of the display to toggle Allow Applications to Request to Track.

VERIFY THE PRIVACY PREFERENCES

The iPad is constructed to safeguard your information and privacy. Apps can be granted or denied permission to trace your activity across the websites and applications of third parties.

To enable applications to request to monitor your activity, navigate to Settings  > Privacy and Security, select Tracking, and toggle Allow Applications to Request to monitor to the on position (green).

MAINTAIN CONTACT WITH FAMILY AND ACQUAINTANCES

iPad facilitates communication with loved ones through video conversations and text messages, the ability to create a shared picture library, and even the ability to view movies or listen to music together.

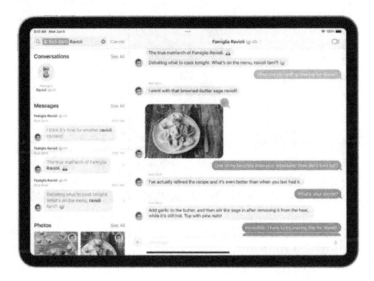

A Messages interface that displays a conversational group

COMMENCE A GROUP DISCUSSION

You can communicate with a group of individuals simultaneously, such as family members, via message.

Tap the Compose icon in the Messages application, enter the names of the recipients, and then send the initial message.

In addition to sharing photographs and videos and collaborating on documents, group conversation participants may also view a movie and listen to music.

A FaceTime conference conversation involving four participants. The FaceTime controls, such as the Speaker, the camera, Mute, Share, as well as End icons, are located in the bottom left corner. In the lower right corner, a tiny rectangle contains the image of the caller.

Perform a video contact

Make video conversations with family and acquaintances via FaceTime.

Click New FaceTime close to the very top of the screen in the FaceTime application 📹 , then enter the name of the recipient before tapping.

Additional participants can be added to a FaceTime conversation at any time, including family and acquaintances. Tap the display to reveal the controls, and then click Add People via the More Info icon ⓘ located at the very top of the controls.

A FaceTime display containing a video communication featuring an individual and a canine companion

Transmit a video communication

When someone is unreachable via the FaceTime app, it is possible to convey your precise thoughts through a video message that you can record.

Tap Record Video, then record your message while the countdown timer (from 5 to 1) is active. To send, tap the Up icon.

Tap Video when a recorded message is received to play it.

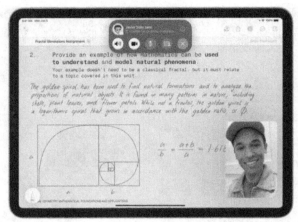

A FaceTime conversation displaying video content and SharePlay controls.

COLLABORATIVELY OBSERVE, ENGAGE AND WORK TOGETHER

During FaceTime conversations, you can utilize applications, play games, or view videos with SharePlay, which is in the FaceTime app.

Launch a supported application during a FaceTime conversation to initiate SharePlay, then select Play to share alongside everyone.

An image displaying photographs of a gathering of acquaintances

ESTABLISH A COLLABORATIVE PHOTO ALBUM

The shared photo library provided by iCloud allows you to share videos and pictures with up to five additional family members or acquaintances via the Photos application . All users are permitted to add, amend, and annotate photos, as well as peruse the featured photos, Photos widget, and shared pictures in their memories.

For all members to utilize the iCloud Shared Picture Library, iCloud Photos must be enabled. To do so, navigate to Settings > [your username] > iCloud > pictures, and then toggle Sync on for this iPad. To begin, select Shared Library from the menu.

PERSONALIZE THE WORKPLACE

By utilizing the iPad's multitasking capabilities, it is possible to simultaneously use and swiftly transition between multiple applications. Stage Manager is an application that enables users to manipulate the dimensions, overlap, and group app windows on their supported iPad models.

App Switcher displays a variety of recently utilized applications.

INTERACT WITH APPLICATIONS ON AN IPAD

By utilizing the Dock while working on one application, it is possible to launch another application without having to return to the Home Screen. Swipe up slightly from the bottom margin of the screen to disclose the Dock located at the bottom of your display, then select the desired app from the current app.

To rapidly navigate between open applications, swipe the screen's bottom boundary to the left or right.

The Maps application is launched on the right edge of the screen, while the Keynote application is active on the left. A divider that can be adjusted between applications is utilized for resizing the Split View.

COMPARING TWO APPLICATIONS SIDE BY SIDE

You can activate a second app adjacent to the one you are currently using on the screen. Tap the Split View option after tapping the Multitasking Controls icon at the top of the screen. When the main screen appears, select the second application you wish to launch. The second application is displayed adjacent to the first.

To modify the dimensions of the two applications positioned on the screen, tap and hold the application divider, followed by a leftward or rightward movement.

Keynote occupies the entire display. On the right edge of the display, a SlideOver display contains the Maps application.

PRIORITIZE A PARTICULAR APP OVER ANOTHER

To transition between two applications while working in one, you can minimize the first app window's size to the point where it floats above the second app. To launch a second application, select the Multitasking Controls icon at the very top of the screen, then slide over to access the Home Screen. As the second application launches in full screen, the initial application floats on top of it.

To relocate the Slide Over program to the opposite side of the display, use the Multitasking Controls icon located at the window's top and drag it to the left or right.

A display on an iPad with Stage Manager active. Other recent applications are displayed in an array on the screen's left-hand side, with the current instances positioned in the center.

GAIN A GREATER UNDERSTANDING OF THE STAGE MANAGER

Using Stage Manager on compatible iPad designs, you can simultaneously observe all of your open applications on the screen and navigate between them with ease.

Slide down from the upper-right corner to access Control Centre, then select the Stage Manager icon⁝☐ to activate it.

APPLY THE APPLE PENCIL TO MORE

Apple Pencil grants users an entirely new iPad experience by enabling annotation, drawing, marking, and editing in their daily-used applications.

A Quick Note appears in the lower-right corner of a Pages document.

Compose a brief note

You can write down ideas as well as add links to Quick Note on your iPad regardless of the task at hand. Commence writing by swiping the Apple Pencil across the lower-right corner of the iPad to the selected note.

A Freeform board containing plant illustrations with drawing instruments located at the bottom.

Compile concepts in Freeform

Utilizing the Freeform application , users can view and collaborate on their ideas in a pliable canvas. FaceTime allows you to collaborate with a friend on drawings, generate large ideas, and diagram new projects. Tap the newest Board icon ⬜ to generate a new board, and then begin sketching with the Apple Pencil. Utilize implements such as a highlighter, calligraphy pen, and watercolor brush to manifest your thoughts onto a board; the sole constraint is your creativity.

The addition of a title to a Keynote slideshow. As Apple Pencil is used to handwrite text, the characters are converted to typed text.

Convert handwritten to typed form

You may utilize the Apple Pencil to transcribe your handwritten words into typed text in any designated area. Your handwriting is directly converted to text on your iPad, ensuring the confidentiality of your writing.

Navigate to Settings > Apple Pencil and activate Scribble.

An image captured of a Pages doc containing red marker-annotated comments.

Annotate a screenshot

Capture and annotate a screenshot expeditiously to provide concise feedback on a group project. Swiping using the Apple Pencil toward the bottom-left area of the iPad will capture a screenshot. Click the thumbnail that appears momentarily in a corner of the display, then add your notes using the drawing tools. By tapping the Share icon⬆️, you can distribute your feedback.

PERSONALIZE AN IPAD FOR A CHILD

The iPad can be configured with controls for parents and features that are suitable for children. Establish inactivity and app limits, safeguard the vision health of your child, shield them from explicit images, approve purchases, and more. With Guided Access, you can even keep the kid focused on a single application.

The Create a Child's Account screen, includes input fields for the child's given name, last name, as well as date of birth.

APPLE ID CREATION FOR YOUR OFFSPRING

You can construct an Apple ID for your child as an alternative to granting them unauthorized access to your private data through the use of a shared account. Parents can easily configure age-based privacy settings from their devices if they are the family organizer. This allows them to utilize various Apple services such as Family Sharing, Messages, and the App Store. Tap Add Member from the Settings > Family menu, followed by Create Child Account.

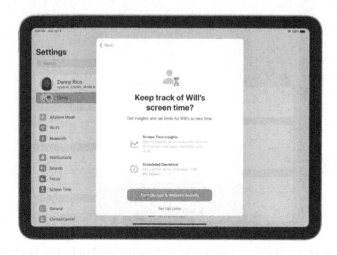

A display containing a description of functionalities for monitoring a child's screen time, including scheduled leisure.

ESTABLISH LIMITS ON SCREEN TIME

You can impose restrictions on inactivity and apps on your child's iPad using Screen Time. Navigate to Settings ⚙ > Family, select Screen Time, and then tap your child's name.

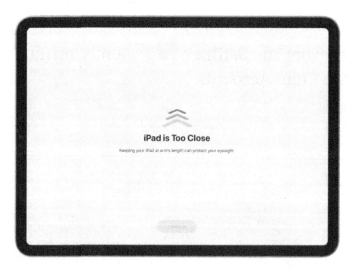

A display that indicates the iPad is approaching closely and recommends maintaining a distance of arm's length. As the iPad approaches a greater distance, the Continue icon appears at the bottom, allowing the user to return to the earlier screen.

CONTRIBUTE TO SAFEGUARDING YOUR CHILD'S VISUAL HEALTH

Screen Distance, which is accessible for iPad Pro models using Face ID, notifies your child when the iPad is held too near for a long amount of time, thereby reducing eye strain as well as the risk of developing myopia. Tap your child's name in the Family section of the Settings menu, followed by Screen Time and Screen Distance.

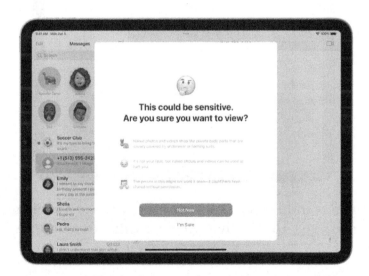

A display indicating that a particular message might contain sensitive images. There are options to seek assistance or disregard the warning at the bottom.

SAFEGUARD YOUR CHILD AGAINST EXPLICIT RECORDINGS AND PHOTOGRAPHS

Nudity can be detected in photographs and videos on an iPad before their transmission or viewing via Messages , AirDrop, and other applications. Your child can obtain age-appropriate guidance and resources to assist them in making a safe decision. Tap your child's name in the Family section of the Setting s menu, followed by Screen Time and Communication Safety.

The Settings interface, which displays features such as Apple Cash and Ask to Buy that are accessible to an adolescent family member

APPLE CASH SETUP (U.S. ONLY)

You can enable Apple Cash for the children in the family sharing group so they can transfer money in Messages and make purchases. You can also secure your child's account, restrict the recipients of their money transfers, and receive notifications regarding their transactions. select the name of your child in Settings  > Family, then select Apple Cash. Subsequently, adhere to the on-screen prompts.

The configuration page for a Guided Entry session. Before beginning the session, you may deactivate specific regions of the display by circling them.

REINFORCE YOUR CHILD'S FOCUS

You can assist your child in maintaining focus and avoiding interruptions by limiting them to just one app, such as Freeform or Books, through the use of Guided Access. Navigate to the Settings >

HIGHLIGHTS OF THE IPADOS 17

Lock Screen. Customize the lock screen of your iPad with new background options, engaging widgets, as well as fonts in the dimensions and hues of your choosing. Observe Live Activities to obtain real-time updates on matters such as the status of your meal delivery or the score of a game.

The time, date, and location are displayed at the center of the iPad Lock Screen. The following widgets are arranged from top to bottom on the left edge of the screen: Apple Pencil Battery, Clock, Calendar, Reminders, and Weather.

Input-capable widgets. Including interactive features on the Home Screen as well as the Lock Screen enhances the utility of widgets. Simply tapping a widget will accomplish duties such as regulating the lighting in your living room, marking off a to-do thing, or launching a new podcast program.

The iPad's home interface. The elements for Weather, Notifications, Home, Music, as well as Photos are located at the very top of the display. Widgets for Home, Reminders, and Music that present interactive elements.

Communication (messages). It is possible to request or share the location of an acquaintance within a Messages conversation. Presently, audio communications are transcribed, enabling immediate reading and subsequent listening. You can locate the desired message more quickly by combining categories to refine your search.

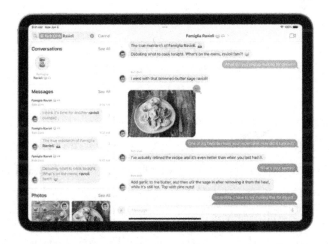

A conversation is displayed by the Messages application on the right edge of the screen. The search field, located in the upper-left corner of the screen, is populated with an assortment of search terms. Results from searches for discussions, messages, and images containing the specified search terms are displayed beneath the search field.

Adhesive stickers. Apply Stickers to screenshots, photographs, and more. Stickers can be added in any location where the on-screen keyboard and markup tools are accessible. Messages decals can be generated from Memoji, your photographs, or Live photographs.

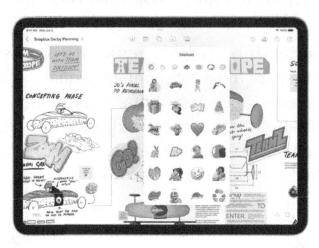

A board created in the Freeform application. When the Media icon is clicked, a menu containing sticker options appears.

FaceTime. You can currently leave a video or audio file message for FaceTime users who do not respond to your calls. Utilize hand gestures during FaceTime calls to generate screen-filling reactions such as hearts, confetti, and pyrotechnics. Transfer FaceTime conversations between an Apple TV and an iPad.

FaceTime is displaying a video message.

Health concerns. The Health application has been optimized for the larger screen of the iPad. Among other features, you can monitor your menstrual cycle, create medication reminders, evaluate health trends as well as highlights, and utilize interactive charts. Additionally, you can monitor your emotional state to increase your self-awareness and gain access to mental health resources.

The Health application Summary view, which provides information regarding sleep, activity, earpiece audio levels, as well as more

Screen Separation. Screen Time's Screen Distance function, which prompts you to relocate your iPad further away after prolonged use of one that is closer than 12 inches, can assist in the preservation of your vision. Assist in safeguarding your visual well-being with Display Distance on iPad.

The keypad. Temporarily highlighted autocorrected words indicate what has been altered; to return to the original word, simply tap. While typing, predictive text appears inline; to complete a word or sentence, simply press the Space bar (not available in all regions or countries).

A dialogue within the Messages application. The word "chill" is highlighted as it is input into the text field located at the bottom of the screen. An arrow is shown above the highlighted word "chillax," suggesting that "chill" be substituted with "chillax."

A Visual Ascent. Pause a video at any frame to implement Visual Look Up. Visual Look Up is capable of identifying foods in images and videos and recommending related recipes. Additionally, visual lookup data is accessible for objects that are lifted from the backgrounds of photographs.

Images and videos. Like a family member or acquaintance, an iPad can identify and categorize pets in the People and Pets album. When updating the focal point of a portrait, select a new one. It is possible to reorder photographs and videos inside a memory as well as add any image from the photo libraries to a memory.

Safari. Implement distinct profiles for various subjects, such as professional and personal, to maintain a categorized browsing experience. Mail autofill verifications are populated in-app, eliminating the need to exit Safari to input them. Additionally, it is possible to distribute passwords for a collection of accounts among trusted family and friends.

The Tab or Group menu is visible to the upper left of a search field in Safari. Selecting Profile from the menu's bottom brings up a menu containing the following options: personal, school, as well as work.

Protection and privacy. Protections against sensitive photos and videos, including those sent and received via AirDrop, Contacts Posters, the system-wide picture selector, and FaceTime messages, have been added to Communication Safety. Using Sensitive Content Warning, you have the option to obscure sensitive images and videos before viewing them. Lockdown Mode enhancements contribute to defense against sophisticated cyberattacks.

Freeform in nature. Utilize novel drawing implements during ideation on a board, such as a calligraphy pen, watercolor brush, highlighter, variable-width pencil, and ruler. Observe the activity of your collaborators using Follow Along—the content that they observe as they navigate the board is displayed on your screen.

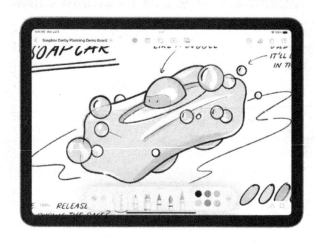

Handwritten text and illustrations on a freeform paper. The drawing instruments are displayed at the bottom.

Ensuring accessibility. Personal Voice enables individuals with speech loss to generate a voice that resembles their own and utilize it in conjunction with Live Speeches to conduct conversations and phone interactions.

A magnifying glass. Point and Speak enables individuals with limited vision or blindness to interact more easily with tangible items that feature text labels.

News. Apple News+ auditory stories are accessible via the Podcasts app, and subscribers have access to daily crossword challenges in the News app. Access subscriber-only materials in Podcast on iPad and solve crossword challenges in the Apple News application on iPad.

A few notes. Review PDFs as well as scans of assignments, presentations, and research papers, as well with ease, directly in your note. Links can be incorporated to establish connections between related notes, such as a list of suggested establishments or a trip itinerary.

Such as reminders. Grocery lists facilitate purchasing by automatically categorizing products. Additionally, headings can be used to divide lists into sections, and a fresh Column View aligns sections adjacently to assist with task visualization.

A Reminders grocery list in which the categories are arranged in columns. Locate the New Item icon in the lower-left corner.

Home. Activity History displays the time and identity of each secure and unlock operation. Additionally, recent activity for your security system, contact sensors, and garage doors is displayed.

Acquire strategies for iPadOS 17The Tips application consistently updates with fresh recommendations to optimize the performance of your iPad.

ACTIVATE AND CONFIGURE IPAD

Online connectivity is required to activate and configure the new iPad. Additionally, iPad setup is possible via a USB connection to a computer. You may transfer your data from an existing iPhone, iPad, or Android device to your newly purchased iPad.

Note: For configuration instructions, if the iPad is deployed and managed by a business, school, or other entity, consult an administrator or teacher.

READINESS FOR ASSEMBLY

To ensure a seamless setup process, ensure the following items are readily accessible:

❖ A Wi-Fi network connection (for which the network's name and password may be required) or cellular data connection provided by a carrier (for Wi-Fi + Cellular variants)

❖ Your Apple ID as well as password; setup will prompt you to create an Apple ID if you do not already have one.

❖ Credit or debit cards are required account details, should you wish to add a card during Apple Pay setup.

❖ A backup of the gadget or your previous iPad, if you are transferring data to the new device.

Advice: Should you encounter an insufficient amount of storage capacity to back out the device, iCloud will provide you with an unlimited amount of space for a maximum of three weeks via the date of purchase of your iPad, at no cost, for completing a temporary backup. Navigate to Settings> General > Move or Reset [device] on your previous device. Once you have selected Get Started, adhere to the on-screen prompts.

❖ Android device, if Android content is being transferred.

ACTIVATE AND CONFIGURE YOUR IPAD

❖ Maintain the top button pressed and held until the logo of Apple appears.

An icon denoted by a green arrow in the upper-right corner of the iPad.

If the iPad will not power on, the battery may need to be recharged. Consult the Apple Help article if the iPad is locked or will not power on for further assistance.

Triple-clicking the Home button (on iPad models with a Home button) or the top icon (on other iPad models) will activate VoiceOver, the screen reader, for those who are blind or have impaired vision. Zoom can also be activated by double-tapping the display with three fingertips.

❖ Perform one of the subsequent actions:
  ✓ Quick Start allows you to have a different iPhone or iPad running iOS 11, iPad operating system 13, or a later version set up as your fresh one automatically. Adhere to the on-screen guidance and bring the two devices near one another to duplicate numerous settings, preferences, as well as iCloud Keychain securely. You can restore the

remaining data and content from the iCloud backup to your new device.

If both devices are running iOS 12.4, iPad operating system 13, and a later version, it is also possible to wirelessly transfer all data from the previous device to the new one. Maintain a physical connection between your devices and ensure they are connected until the migration is finished.

Data can also be transmitted between devices via a wired connection. Consult the Apple Help article Transferring Data to a Newer iPad or iPhone Using Quick Start.

✓ Select Manual Setup, then adhere to the setup instructions displayed on-screen.

TRANSITION FROM AN ANDROID TO AN IPAD

Using the App to Transfer Data to the iOS application, you can migrate data from your Android device to your new iPad during the initial setup process.

Note: To use Shift to iOS after setup is complete, you must either delete your iPad and restart the process, or manually transfer your data.

❖ Install the shift to iOS application from the article by Apple Support titled Transfer from Android to the iPad or iPhone on a device running Android 4.0 or later.

❖ Utilize your iPad to perform the following:
    ✓ Assist with the preparation process.

- ✓ Tap From Android on the Move Your Apps and Data interface.
- ❖ Perform the following operations on the Android device:
  - ✓ Activate Wi-Fi.
  - ✓ Launch the Transfer files to the iOS application.
  - ✓ Follow the instructions displayed on-screen.

UNLOCK AND WAKE THE IPAD

When not in use, the iPad powers down to conserve energy, locks for security purposes, and enters sleep mode. You can rapidly activate and wake the iPad when you need to begin using it again.

Restart the iPad

To rouse an iPad, perform one of the following actions:

- ❖ Utilize the upper tab.

An icon denoted by a green arrow in the upper-right corner of the iPad.

- ❖ Tap the display (models supported).

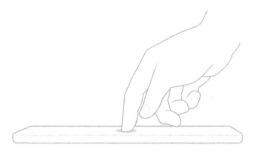

By touching the display, one can awaken the iPad.

IPAD UNLOCKING USING FACE ID

❖ Following a tap, take a quick gander at your iPad. The animation of the lock icon from locked to open signifies that the iPad has been opened.

❖ From the bottom of the display, swipe upward.

To re-lock the iPad, tap its upper icon. iPad will autonomously close after approximately one minute without contact with the display. With Attention Aware Features enabled in Settings > Face ID & Passcode, the iPad will remain illuminated and will not dim or lock while attention is being detected.

IPAD UNLOCKING VIA TOUCH ID

If Touch ID was not activated during setup on your iPad, refer to the section titled "Set up Touch Identification on iPad."

❖ Utilize the finger that was registered with the Touch ID sensor to press the Home key on an iPad equipped with such a feature.

The Touch ID (Home) sensor located on the underside of the iPad.

❖ iPad Air (4th version and later), iPad mini (6th version), and iPad (10th generation): Utilize the finger that was registered with the Touch ID finger to gently press the top button.

An icon denoted by a green arrow in the upper-right corner of the iPad.

To re-lock the iPad, tap its upper icon. iPad will autonomously close after approximately one minute without contact with the display.

IPAD UNLOCK USING A PASSCODE

If the iPad setup did not include the creation of a passcode

❖ Swipe upwards from the bottom of the screen that appears (on iPad models without a Home button) or press the Home key (on iPad models with a Home button).

❖ Make use of the passcode.

To re-lock the iPad, tap its upper icon. iPad will autonomously close after approximately one minute without contact with the display.

CONFIGURE IPAD CELLULAR SERVICE (WI-FI + CELLULAR MODELS)

You may enroll in a cellular data package if you own a Wi-Fi Plus Cellular model. This allows you to maintain an internet connection even when you are not in range of a Wi-Fi network.

A cellular connection necessitates the use of a SIM card and a carrier-issued wireless data plan. The following SIM card varieties are supported by iPad:

❖ (On iPad versions that support eSIM; availability varies by country and region).
❖ Constant SIM

Specific iPad models are 5G network-capable.

Configure an eSIM

For iPad models with an eSIM, cellular service activation is possible through the iPad itself. Additionally, it may be possible to utilize an iPad while traveling internationally by subscribing to cellular service alongside an authorized carrier in the destination country or region. Not all regions or countries offer this option, and not all service providers support it.

❖ Navigate to the Settings⚙ menu and select Cellular Data.

❖ Perform one of the subsequent actions:
  ✓ Configure the initial cellular subscription on the iPad: Once you have chosen a carrier, adhere to the on-screen prompts.
  ✓ To add a second cellular plan, select Add The new Plan.
  ✓ Scan a carrier-supplied QR code to Tap Other, then manually enter the information or position the iPad to ensure the QR code supplied by the provider appears in the frame. A carrier-issued confirmation code may be required for entry.

Alternatively, if supported by your carrier, you may activate the cell phone service via their app. Download the app for your carrier from the App Store, and then use it to buy a cellular plan.

iPad users are permitted to retain and utilize a maximum of one e-SIM at a time. Tap the desired plan (below SIMs) in Setting > Cellular Data to change to a different eSIM.

Present a tangible SIM card

Carriers offer nano-SIM cards for sale.

❖ To expel the SIM tray, insert a paper pin or SIM ejection tool (not provided) into the tiny opening in the tray and press in toward the iPad.

To expel and remove the SIM tray from the iPad, a clip of paper or SIM ejection tool is pushed into the tiny aperture of the tray located on the opposite side of the device.

Note: Depending on the iPad model and country or region, the SIM compartment may have a different form or be oriented differently.

❖ Detach the iPad's compartment.
❖ The SIM card should be inserted into the receptacle. The orientation is determined by the angle of the apex.

To expel and remove the SIM tray from the iPad, a paper clip and SIM ejection tool is pushed into the tiny aperture of the tray located on the left edge of the device.

❖ Reinstall the tray into the iPad.
❖ If a PIN was previously configured on the SIM card, enter it with care when prompted.
Avoid making any attempt to predict a SIM PIN. SIMs that are incorrectly guessed can become perpetually locked, preventing carrier-provided cellular data access until a replacement is obtained.

Consult the article on Apple Support titled "Utilizing a SIM PIN on an iPhone or iPad."

ADMINISTRATION OF CELLULAR DATA COMMUNICATION

❖ Navigate to the Settings menu and select Cellular Data.
❖ Perform one of the following:
  ✓ To limit all data transmissions to Wi-Fi, deactivate cellular data.
  ✓ To enable or disable roaming and LTE, select Cellular Data Options.
  ✓ To activate Personal Hotspot, select Set Up Private Hotspot (offered by select carriers) and proceed with the instructions displayed on-screen.
  ✓ Tap Carrier Services or Manage [account name] to administer your mobile account.

LINK THE IPAD TO THE WEB

Establish a connection between your iPad and the internet via a Wi-Fi network that is accessible. The models with Wi-Fi + Cellular are also capable of establishing cellular network connections to the Internet.

SYNC THE IPAD WITH A WI-FI NETWORK

❖ Navigate to Settings ⚙ > Wi-Fi and activate the feature.
❖ Tap any of the options below:

✓ If prompted, enter the password for the network.
✓ An additional feature is that it joins a covert network. The password, security type, and name of the covert network should be entered.

IOS is linked to a Wi-Fi connection when the Wi-Fi icon becomes visible at the very top of the display. (To confirm this, launch Safari and navigate to a web page.) When the iPad is repositioned to the same location, it reconnects.

Participate in a private hot spot

Utilize the cellular internet connection of an iPhone or iPad (Wi-Fi + Cellular) that is sharing a Private Hotspot.

❖ Navigate to Settings ⚙ > Wi-Fi and select the device's name that will be used to share the personal hotspot.
❖ When prompted for an identification code on your iPad, input the password displayed on the device by accessing the Personal Hotspot under Settings ⚙ > Cellular > Private Hotspot.

IPADS THAT ARE COMPATIBLE WITH CELLULAR NETWORKS (WI-FI PLUS CELLULAR VARIANTS)

In the absence of a Wi-Fi network, your iPad will connect automatically to the cellular data network on your carrier. If the iPad is unable to communicate, verify the following:

- ❖ Confirm that the SIM card has been unlocked and activated. iPad cellular service configuration (Wi-Fi + Cellular variants).
- ❖ Navigate to the Settings menu and select Cellular Data.
- ❖ Confirm that mobile data is operational.

When an internet connection is required, the iPad proceeds as follows, sequentially, until a connection is established:

- ❖ Attempts to establish a connection to a most recently accessible Wi-Fi network
- ❖ Presents a list of nearby Wi-Fi networks and establishes a connection with the one selected.
- ❖ Connects to the cellular data network of your carrier (Wi-Fi + Cellular variants).

iPads that support 5G may utilize cellular data over 5G rather than Wi-Fi. If so, the phrase Using 5G Wireless For Internet appears beneath the name of the Wi-Fi network. Tap the Info icon adjacent to the network's name, followed by Use Wi-Fi for Internet, to revert to Wi-Fi

Apps and services that require an internet connection via Wi-Fi might send data over the cellular network of your carrier, incurring additional charges.

SIGN IN WITH APPLE ID TO YOUR IPAD

Apple's services like the Application Store, iTunes Store, iTunes Literature, Apple Music, FaceTime, iCloud, and iMessage can be accessed through your Apple ID.

Entering your Apple ID to log in

If you failed to log in during configuration, proceed as follows:

- ❖ Navigate to the Settings menu.
- ❖ To log in to your iPad, select Sign in
- ❖ Enter your password and Apple ID.
  You may create an Apple ID if you do not already have one.
- ❖ When two-factor authentication is used to defend your account, you must input the six-digit verifying code.

MODIFY YOUR APPLE ID CONFIGURATION

- ❖ Navigate to the [your name] setting.
- ❖ Perform one of the following:
  - ✓ Please revise your contact details.
  - ✓ Make the password change
  - ✓ Modify the Account Recovery Contacts list.
  - ✓ Implement iCloud
  - ✓ Manage and access your subscriptions
  - ✓ Modify your billing address or payment methods.
  - ✓ Oversee household sharing

HOW TO USE ICLOUD ON IPAD

iCloud automatically updates your pictures, videos, files, backups, and other media across all of your devices while storing them in a secure location.

Additionally, you can share pictures, calendars, notes, a folder, and files with family and friends via iCloud. iCloud grants users access to an email account as well as 5 GB of complimentary data storage.

Certain iCloud features require a minimum system configuration. The regional or national accessibility of iCloud as well as its functionalities may differ.

MODIFY YOUR ICLOUD CONFIGURATION

After logging in with the Apple ID, proceed as follows:

❖ Navigate to iCloud under Settings  > [your name].

The iCloud settings interface displays the iCloud store meter and a selection of iCloud-compatible features, such as Photos, iCloud Drive, or iCloud Backup.

❖ Perform one of the following:
    ✓ View the status of your iCloud storage.
    ✓ Activate the desired features from the menu, including iCloud Backup, Photos, and iCloud Drive.

Ways to use iCloud on an iPad.

How to personalize iCloud features on additional devices is detailed in

iCloud can perform automatic backups of your iPad. See iPad backup.

Additionally, the subsequent data can be retained in iCloud and synchronized consistently across one's iPad along with other Apple devices:

- ❖ Videos and photographs;
- ❖ Documents and records;
- ❖ iCloud Messages
- ❖ Reminders, Contacts, Calendars, and Notes
- ❖ Compatibility with third-party applications and games
- ❖ Messages; see iPad Message Configuration
- ❖ Payment methods and passwords
- ❖ Bookmarks and open tabs in Safari
- ❖ Settings for News, Stocks, and the Weather
- ❖ Data on Health and Residence
- ❖ Verbal memos
- ❖ Favorite maps

You may also perform the subsequent:

- ❖ Share videos and photographs.
- ❖ Documents and folders can be shared via iCloud Drive. On an iPad, navigate to Share folders and files in iCloud Drive.

- ❖ Share the location of a lost device with family and acquaintances using Find My.

ICLOUD+ SUBSCRIPTION

iCloud+ provides all of the same features as iCloud, in addition to premium features such as iCloud Secret Relay, Hide The Email, and support for HomeKit Secure Video. Additionally, it offers ample storage space for your photographs, files, and other data.

A subscription to either iCloud+ or Apple One, which comprises iCloud+ and additional Apple services, is available.

Certain iCloud+ features require a minimum system configuration. The regional or national accessibility of iCloud+ as well as its functionalities may differ.

WHAT IS ICLOUD+ INCLUSIVE OF?

iPad users with an iCloud+ subscription have the following capabilities:

- ❖ Access storage for 50 GB, two hundred GB, or 2 TB.
- ❖ Employ Hide My Email to generate arbitrary, one-of-a-kind email addresses that are forwarded to your inbox.
- ❖ Employing iCloud Private Relay enhances the privacy and security of your web browsing experience
- ❖ Configure your security cameras at home with HomeKit Secured Video to maintain the privacy and security of footage viewed from any location.

❖ To customize iCloud Mail, utilize a custom email domain.

MODIFY, TERMINATE, OR UPGRADE YOUR ICLOUD+ SUBSCRIPTION

❖ Navigate to iCloud under Settings > [your name].
❖ After selecting an option from Change Storage Plan under Manage Account Storage, proceed by following the on-screen prompts.
iCloud+ features and additional iCloud storage are rendered inaccessible upon cancellation of the subscription.

Propose iCloud+

Family Sharing allows you to share iCloud+ with a maximum of five additional family members. Upon accepting the request to share iCloud+, your family members will be granted immediate access to the supplementary storage and features.

Note: To cease sharing iCloud+ alongside a family group, one may quit the family group, terminate the subscription, or disable Family Sharing.

IDENTIFY SETTINGS ON THE IPAD

You can search the Settings application for iPad settings that you wish to modify, including the passcode, notification noises, and more.

❖ Select Settings from the App Library or the Home Screen.

The iPad homepage contains a variety of app icons, one of which is the Settings app indicator, which can be tapped to modify the screen luminance, sound volume, and other settings.

❖ To initiate a search, swipe downward on the sidebar and select the search field located at the top left. Input a desired term, such as "volume," and then select a setting from the menu on the far left of the screen.

The iPad homepage contains a variety of app icons, one of which is the Settings app indicator, which can be tapped to

modify the screen luminance, sound volume, and other settings.

CONFIGURE CALENDAR, EMAIL, AND CONTACT INFORMATION

Besides the pre-installed applications and those utilized with iCloud, the iPad is also compatible with Exchange from Microsoft and a multitude of widely used cloud-based mail, calendar, and contact services. Accounts are available for these services.

CREATING A MAIL ACCOUNT

❖ Add an account by navigating to Settings ⚙ > Mail > Accounts.
❖ Perform one of the subsequent actions:
  ✓ After selecting a service, such as Microsoft Exchange or iCloud, input your account information.
  ✓ Select Other, then select Add Mail Account, followed by the input of your account details.

CREATING AN ACCOUNT FOR CONTACTS

❖ Select Add Account from the Settings ⚙ > Contact > Accounts menu.
❖ Perform one of the subsequent actions:
  ✓ After selecting a service, such as Microsoft Exchange or iCloud, input your account information.
  ✓ Proceed by selecting Other, followed by Add LDAP Account and Add CardDAV User (if

supported by your organization), and finally input the server as well as account details.

CREATING A CALENDAR ACCOUNT

❖ Add an account by navigating to Settings > Calendar > Accounts.
❖ Perform one of the subsequent actions:
    ✓ Select the service: After selecting a service, such as Microsoft Exchange or iCloud, input your account information.
    ✓ Create a schedule entry: select Other, then select Add CalDAV Account, followed by the input of your server as well as account details.
    ✓ Obtain an iCal (.ics) subscription: Import an existing .ics file from Mail or select Other, then Add Subscribed Calendar, followed by the URL of the .ics file to which you wish to subscribe.

REPLACE THE IPAD'S BATTERY

The iPad is powered by a lithium-ion rechargeable internal battery. At this time, lithium-ion technology offers the most optimal performance for your gadget. Lithium-ion batteries have an increased energy density, are lighter, charge more rapidly, and have a longer lifespan than conventional battery technologies.

For comprehensive insights into the functioning of your battery to optimize its performance, we recommend visiting the official website for Apple Lithium-ion Batteries.

CONCERNING THE BATTERY CHARGE

A lightning bolt-shaped icon for the battery indicates that it is charging.

The battery's level or recharging status is indicated by the icon located in the upper-right area of the status bar. While synchronizing or using the iPad, the battery may require additional time to charge.

An image of a virtually depleted battery may appear on an iPad when the device's power is extremely low, indicating that it may take up to ten minutes to recharge before it can be used again. The screen may be inactive for a maximum of two minutes before the appearance of the low-battery icon if the iPad is exceedingly low on capacity when the charging process commences.

CHARGING THE BATTERY

To charge the battery in your iPad, perform the following:

❖ By utilizing the supplied cable and power adapter, link the iPad to an electrical receptacle

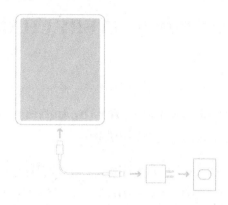

The iPad was powered by an adapter that was inserted into an electrical receptacle.

HOW TO MAKE A CONNECTION BETWEEN AN IPAD AND A COMPUTER USING A CABLE

It is imperative to have your computer powered on before connecting your iPad to it; otherwise, the battery may deplete rather than recharge. Ensure the iPad is charging by examining the battery icon for a charging icon.

If the power supply of the computer or Mac is insufficient to charge the iPad, the status bar will display the message "Not Charging."

Connecting your iPad to your keyboard to charge it is not recommended unless the keyboard features a high-power USB interface.

HOW TO DISPLAY THE BATTERY LIFE IN PERCENTAGE

The remaining battery life of your iPad is displayed in the status indicator. In addition, one may incorporate a widget into the Home Screen to monitor the battery levels for connected accessories, such as AirPods, the Apple Pencil, and other devices.

THE IPAD'S BATTERY PERCENTAGE DISPLAYED IN THE STATUS PANE

In the Settings menu, select Battery, and then enable Battery Percentage.

EXAMINE THE BATTERY UTILIZATION

To observe the impact of your iPad's usage on its battery life, navigate to Settings > Battery

Data regarding the utilization and activity of your battery is displayed for the previous twenty-four hours and a maximum of ten days.

❖ Suggestions and observations: You may gain knowledge regarding circumstances or utilization patterns that result in energy consumption on the iPad. Potential recommendations for reducing energy usage may also be presented. Tapping a suggestion will take you to the setting associated with that suggestion.

❖ Last Charged: Indicates the time since the battery was disconnected and the extent to which it was last charged.

❖ Displays the battery level, recharging intervals, and durations during which the iPad was in Low-Power mode or the power had been critically low over the past twenty-four hours.

- ❖ The battery usage graph (over the past 10 days) illustrates the daily percentage of battery consumption.
- ❖ Activity graph: Displays activity over time, segmented by screen state (on or off).
- ❖ Displays the entire amount of activity that occurred during the specified time interval, including both the periods when the display was on and off. The final 10 Days view provides daily averages.
- ❖ Displays the percentage of the battery that was consumed by each application during the specified period.
- ❖ Activity by App: Displays the duration of use for each application during the specified time interval.

Note: To view battery data for a particular hour or day, select the corresponding time interval on the graph. To deselect a data point, touch beyond the graph.

Charge cycles and battery life vary based on usage and configuration. Service or recycling of the iPad battery is the responsibility of Apple along with an Apple Approved Service Provider.

UTILIZE THE LOW-POWER MODE TO CONSERVE BATTERY LIFE

Low Power Mode decreases the power consumption of your iPad when the battery is low. It enhances performance for critical operations such as telephony and telephony reception, email and message transmission and reception, internet access, and more.

Low Power Mode restricts the refresh rate of displays equipped with ProMotion technology to sixty frames per second.

Keep in mind that certain operations on your iPad may be slowed down while in Low Battery Mode.

If the iPad automatically enters Low Power Mode, it exits the mode once the battery is charged to 80% capacity.

ENABLE OR DISABLE LOW-POWER MODE

Low Power Mode is an automatic function that activates when the battery's power level is low as well as deactivates when it reaches a predetermined charge level.

To manually enable or disable Low Power Mode, employ one of the subsequent procedures:

❖ Go to the Settings menu and select Battery.
❖ Launch Control Centre, followed by tapping the icon labeled Low Power Mode.
(To add the Low Power Options button to Control Centre, navigate to Settings > Control Centre and select the Insert icon next to Low Battery Mode if it is not already present.)

CHAPTER TWO

CORE ASPECTS

LEARN FUNDAMENTAL IPAD INTERACTION GESTURES

Use a few straightforward gestures to operate the iPad and its applications: tap, touch as well as hold, swipe, navigate, and magnify.

SYMBOL	GESTURES
●	Tap. Touch an object on the display briefly with one finger. To launch an application, for instance, touch the app's icon on the Homepage Screen.
◉	Hold and touch. When an item appears on the screen, press it until an action is taken. For instance, when the Home Screen wallpaper is touched and held, the application symbols start to vibrate.
↑	Utilize a swipe. Rapidly navigate with one finger throughout the display. Slide left on the main screen, for instance, to view additional applications.
↕	Proceed to scroll. Navigate the display with a single finger without raising it. To view additional items, for instance, in pictures, one can drag the list up or down. To scroll rapidly, swipe the screen; to halt scrolling, contact the display.

	Zoom. Position two fingertips adjacent to one another on the display. Move them toward one another to achieve a zoom-out, or apart to achieve a zoom-in. Additionally, you can double-tap a webpage or image to enlarge it and double-click again to reduce its size. To zoom in or out of Maps, double-click or hold, and afterward drag up or down, respectively.

MASTER ADVANCED IPAD GESTURES FOR INTERACTION

The following is a comprehensive list of the gestures that can be utilized on any iPad model to access controls, navigate to the main screen, and transition between recent applications. As detailed in the subsequent table, an iPad featuring a Home button implements a few gestures differently.

GESTURE	DESCRIPTION
	Return home. Swipe upwards at any time from the bottom margin of the display to access the Home Screen.

	Gain rapid access to controls. To access the Control Centre, swipe lower from the upper-right corner; touching and holding a control will disclose additional options. To modify or add controls, navigate to Settings > Control Centre.
	Commence using the App Switcher. Lift your finger after pausing in the center of the screen and swiping up from the lower edge. Swipe right to navigate through the open applications, then select the desired application.
	Move between active applications. Utilize the bottom edge swipe buttons (left and right) to rapidly navigate between open applications. (Swipe with a minor arc on an iPad with the Home button.)
	Launch the Dock inside a program. Pause while swiping upward from the bottom margin of the display to unveil the Dock. To launch an additional application rapidly, select its icon in the Dock.
	Apply Siri. Conversely, you may also initiate a request by pressing and holding the top icon while saying "Siri" or "Hey Siri." (To initiate a request on an iPad equipped with a button for Home, hold down the Home icon while speaking.) Subsequently, release the button.

	Employ an accessible shortcut. Click the upper icon three times. (Triple-click the Home icon on an iPad.)
	Annotate the screen. Concurrently press and promptly depress the top button along with either volume control. (On an iPad equipped with a button for Home, hold and let go of the top icon and the button for Home simultaneously.)
	Turn the device off. To turn it off, hold the top icon and the bottom button simultaneously until sliders show up, then drag the upper slider. (Press and hold the upper button on an iPad equipped with the Home button until sliders appear.) Alternatively, navigate to Settings > General > Shutdown.
	Compel a reload. Hold the top button down until the logo of Apple appears, after which press and quickly drop the volume button adjacent to it, press as well as quickly release the second volume button, and finally hold down the top button. The volume controls for the iPad mini (6th iteration) are located in the upper left corner.

MODIFY THE VOLUME SETTING

Change the volume of notifications, sound effects, songs, and other media using the audio controls on the iPad. (Such as the model may specify, that the volume controls are located on the top or side of the device.)

Additionally, you can adjust the volume with Siri.

To use Siri, say "Turn up the volume" or "Turn down the volume." Acquire the necessary skills to operate Siri.

It is possible to suppress audio notifications and alerts via the Control Centre.

ADVICE: For critical details regarding the prevention of hearing loss

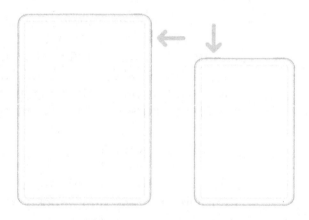

Two distinct iPad variants are displayed frontally. The volume controls are located near the upper-right corner of the model on the left, with the top button in the same location. The volume and touch ID controls are located in the upper left and right corners, respectively, of the model depicted on the right.

The Do Not Disturb feature does not mute the audio of podcasts, music, videos, or television programs.

LOCK ALERT VOLUMES AND THE RINGER

Select Sounds from the Settings⚙ menu, then deactivate Change with Buttons.

VOLUME ADJUSTMENTS IN THE CONTROL CENTRE

Control Centre allows volume adjustments to be made while the iPad has been locked or an application is running.

Launch the Control Centre and drag the volume adjuster to the right or left 🔊

REDUCING HARSH EARPHONE SOUNDS

❖ Navigate to Headphone Safety in Adjustments > Sounds.
❖ Activate Reduce Loud Sound, and then adjust the utmost volume using the slider.
  Note that Screen Time can be implemented to restrict family members from modifying the Reduce Loud Noises setting. Enable privacy and content restrictions by navigating to Setting > Display Time > Content and Privacy Restrictions, then tap Reduce Loud Sounds followed by Don't Allow.

SILENCE THE SOUND ENTIRELY

Maintaining pressure on the Volume Down switch

HOW TO LAUNCH APPLICATIONS

Apps can be launched rapidly from the pages of your Home Screen.

❖ Swipe upward from the screen's bottom margin to access the Home Screen.

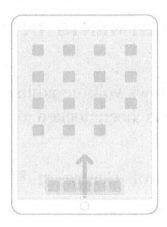

An illustration of accessing the Home Screen by dragging upwards from the bottom margin of the display

❖ To navigate between applications on different Home Screen pages, swipe left or right.

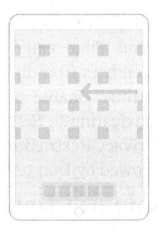

An example of how to navigate through applications on other display pages by swiping

❖ Tap an application's icon on the main screen to launch it.

❖ To access the initial Home Screen page again, use the downward motion from the screen's bottom edge.

FIND YOUR APPLICATIONS IN THE IPAD'S APP LIBRARY

App Library displays your applications in categories including Information & Reading, Productivity & Finance, and Creativity. To facilitate effortless navigation and access, the applications that you utilize most frequently are positioned at the highest level of their classifications and near the very top of the screen.

The iPad's App Library displays the applications in a categorical fashion, including Entertainment, Productivity, Finance, and others.

Notably, the applications in the App Library are ingeniously categorized according to their usage patterns. Apps stored in the App Library can be added to the Home Screen; however, they cannot be relocated to a different category within the App Library.

LAUNCH AN APPLICATION FROM THE APP LIBRARY

❖ To access the App Library, navigate to the homepage and swipe leftward past all the Home Screen pages. Additionally, you can easily access App Library by selecting the App Library icon , which is located to the right of the Dock around the bottom of the screen.

❖ After tapping on the search box at the very top of the display, input the desired application's name. Navigate through the alphabetical list by scrolling.

❖ Tap an app to launch it. Tap the small app symbols within a category in the app library to expand the grouping and reveal all of its applications.

DISPLAY AND CONCEAL HOME SCREEN PAGES

App Library may contain all of your applications, so you may not require as many display pages dedicated to apps. By hiding certain Home Screen pages, the App Library is displayed in closer proximity to the initial Home Screen page. (You can reveal the concealed pages whenever you desire to view them once more.)

❖ Apply pressure to the homepage until the applications start to vibrate.

❖ Tap the dots located at the display's bottom. After thumbnail images of the Home Screen pages, checkmarks are displayed.

❖ To conceal pages, swipe the checkboxes away.
To enable access to concealed pages, swipe to add checkboxes.
❖ Press Done.

By concealing the additional Home Screen pages, it is possible to navigate from the initial Home Screen page to the App Library (and vice versa) using a maximum of two swipes.

Apps downloaded via the App Store that are concealed from the Home Screen may be appended to the App Library rather than the Home Screen.

HOW TO CHANGE HOME SCREEN'S PAGES ARRANGEMENT

You can rearrange the Home Screen pages if you have more than one. You could, for instance, compile your preferred applications onto a single Home Screen page, which you could then designate as your primary Home Screen page.

❖ When the applications on the Home Screen start to flicker, tap and hold the wallpaper.
❖ Tap the dots located at the display's bottom.
After small pictures of your main screen pages, checkmarks are displayed.
❖ Touch and hold each homepage page, then drag it into a new location, to relocate it.
❖ Press Done.

ALTER THE LOCATION FOR DOWNLOADING NEW APPLICATIONS

Users have the option to add newly downloaded applications from the Apple Store to both the main screen and the Application Library, or the App Library exclusively.

❖ Select Settings > App Library & Home Screen.
❖ Select whether new applications should be added to the App Library only or to both the Home Screen as well as App Library.

Note: Enable Show in the App Library to permit app notification icons to be displayed on applications in the App Library.

TRANSFER AN APPLICATION FROM THE LIBRARY OF APPS TO THE HOME SCREEN

Apps from the App Library can be added to the Main Screen unless they are already present.

Press Add to the homepage after touching and holding the application (accessible only if the application is not already on your Home Screen).

App Library and the Home Screen both feature the application.

SWITCHING BETWEEN APPLICATIONS

On an iPad, you can rapidly transition between applications using the Dock, the application Switcher, or a gesture. When you return to the previous state, you can resume exactly where you stopped.

LAUNCH A PROGRAM VIA THE DOCK

Swipe upwards from the bottom side of the screen from any application just until the Dock appears, and then touch the desired application.

Favorite applications are displayed on the Dock's left side, while suggested applications—including those you've recently launched and those currently running on your iOS device or Mac—are presented on the Dock's right side. The dock's rightmost icon provides access to the App Library.

The Home Page with the Dock presents three suggested applications on the right and seven preferred applications on the left. The icon to the Dock's right-hand side launches App Library.

IMPLEMENT AN APP SWITCHER

❖ Perform one of the following to view all open applications, Split View workplaces, and Slide Over apps in the App Switcher:

  ✓ Swipe upward from the bottom of the display, then halt in the center of the screen on all iPad models.

  ✓ Double-tap the Home button on an iPad equipped with one.

App Switcher displays a variety of recently utilized applications.

❖ Swipe right to navigate through the open applications, and then select the desired application or Split View workspace.

To access the Slide Over windows, perform a left swipe and then tap each one to navigate between them.

NAVIGATE BETWEEN OPEN PROGRAMS

To navigate between open applications, perform one of the following actions:

- ❖ Utilize one finger to swipe either left or right along the bottom perimeter of the display. (If your iPad has a Home icon, execute this action by tracing a faint arc.)
- ❖ Four to five digits should be used to swipe to the left or right.

HOW TO COPY AND RELOCATE ITEMS VIA DRAG-AND-DROP

By utilizing drag and drop, it is possible to copy and move text as well as items from one application to another with a finger. For instance, an image can be dragged from Notes to an email. (Not all third-party applications provide drag-and-drop functionality.)

TRANSFER AN OBJECT

- ❖ Hold the object in your hand until it rises (if it is text, choose it beforehand).
- ❖ Transfer it to a different location within the application by dragging it.
  When you drag a lengthy document to the bottom and top, it scrolls automatically.

TRANSFER A FILE BETWEEN ACTIVE APPLICATIONS

- ❖ Access two items in Slide Over or Split View, then contact and press the item till it ascends (select the item beforehand if it is text).
- ❖ Transfer it to another application by dragging it.

The Insert symbol ⊕ appears wherever the item can be dropped as the user drags. When you drag a lengthy document towards the bottom or top, the document scrolls automatically.

Before dragging an item to a fresh note or email, ensure that the freshly created note or email is open so that the item can be dragged to it directly.

A Divided View with an email visible on the right and notes accessible on the left. An image imported from Notes is appended to the email.

WHEN YOU DRAG A LINK INTO A SLIDE-OVER OR SPLIT-VIEW WINDOW

After touching and holding the link till it begins to rise, perform one of the subsequent actions:

❖ To replace the destination of a link in a Slide Over or Split View window, simply drag that link to the desired window.

❖ In the absence of a Split View and Slide Over window, open the destination by dragging the link to either the right or left side of the screen to access the link in Split View, or close to the edge to access the link in Slide Over.

HOW TO COPY AN ITEM TO AN APP FROM THE DOCK OR HOME SCREEN:

❖ Hold the object in your hand until it rises (if it is text, choose it beforehand).
❖ While maintaining control of the object, move upward from the bottom edge of the display with a second finger and hesitate to disclose the Dock or select the Home icon (on an iPad alongside a Home button).
❖ To launch the other application, drag the object over it (while dragging, a phantom image that represents the item appears beneath your finger).
You can navigate to the desired location to drop an item in the application by dragging it over the item (the Insert icon displays wherever you can place the item as you drag). For instance, you can open a note where you wish to place the item by dragging it over the notes list, or you may use a different finger to open another note where you wish to drop the item.

Lift your finger before dragging an item that you change while thinking about relocating, or removing the item from the screen.

SELECTING MULTIPLE ITEMS TO BE RELOCATED

❖ The initial item that is selected is touched and held, then dragged slightly while being held.

❖ While maintaining a single-item grasp, utilize an additional finger to touch the remaining items. Indicated by an insignia is the quantity of selected products.

❖ Combine each object by dragging it together.

If you alter your mind about relocating an item, either remove it from the screen or elevate your finger before dragging it.

HOW TO OPEN TWO OBJECTS IN SPLIT VIEW

On iPad, it is possible to utilize multiple applications simultaneously. To launch two distinct applications or two windows within a single application, partition the display into resizable sections. For instance, simultaneously open Messages as well as Maps using Split View. Or, utilize Split View to simultaneously manage two conversations by utilizing two Messages windows.

OPENING A SECOND APPLICATION IN SPLIT VIEW

❖ Press the Multitasking Settings button (the three-dot icon at the very top of the app ⋯), and finally click the Split View button ▢. To move the current app to the right side of the screen, tap the Right Splitter

View button ![icon]. Alternatively, you can use the Left Splitting View button ![icon] to move the app to the far left of the screen.

The currently running application slides to a side to disclose the main screen and Dock.

❖ Locate the second application you wish to launch in the Dock or on the Home Screen, then tap it.

Both applications manifest in Split View.

Mail is displayed on the far right side of the display, while the Notes application is active on the left. A divider that can be adjusted between applications is utilized to modify the extent of the division.

APP SUBSTITUTION IN SPLIT VIEW

One of the two applications that are currently open in Split View may be substituted with an alternative app.

- Slide down from the Performing Multiple Tasks Controls icon (the three-dot symbol at the very top of the app) in the application you wish to supplant.
  As the app you wish to replace descends, the other app slides to the side, exposing the Home Screen as well as the Dock.
- Locate and select the replacement application from the Home Screen or Dock.
  The two applications are displayed concurrently in Split View.

Tip: On supported models, to obtain additional workspace, navigate to Settings > Display and Brightness, select Display Zoom, and then More Space. This preference enhances the pixel density, facilitating the expansion of app content when utilizing multiple tabs via Stage Manager or Split View.

CHANGING FROM SPLIT VIEW TO SLIDE-OVER

You can transform one of two apps and windows that are currently visible in Split View into a Flip Over window, which is a tiny window that moves ahead of the active one.

To convert a window into a Slide-Over window, press the Multitasking Controls icon ••• located at the top of the window. Subsequently, touch the Slide Over button ⬜, which is located to the right among the three buttons.

REVERT TO THE FULL DISPLAY

In Split View, if you have two applications or windows active, you can hide one to reveal the other in full-screen view. Perform one of the subsequent actions:

❖ Position the center divider at the screen's right or left edge by dragging it.

❖ Press the Enter Complete Screen icon ▢ after tapping the Performing multiple tasks Controls icon ••• at the very top of the application you wish to launch in full screen.

❖ To launch an application in full-screen mode, press and hold the Performing Multiple Tasks Controls icon ••• located at the very top of the application. Lift your finger after dragging the icon and its name to the center of the screen while maintaining its upper edge at the top.

TRANSFORM AN APP WINDOW INTO A SLIDE-OVER WINDOW

You can move an app to a Slide-in window—a tiny window that moves in ahead of a different application or window—and launch another app from behind it while the current app is active. You could, for instance, have Messages active in a SlideOver display while using the photographs application and converse while viewing photographs.

By keeping note of the applications you launch in Slide Over, iPad facilitates the transition between them.

A Photos application occupies the entire display. A Slide Over pane for Messages is displayed on the right edge of the display.

APP LAUNCH VIA SLIDE OVER

❖ Hit the Slide Over icon  after tapping the Multitasking Settings icon ••• at the very top of the screen while using an application.
The currently running application slides to a side to disclose the Home Screen as well as the Dock.

❖ Locate and launch the desired application behind the Slide it Over window.
As the second application launches, the first application displays a Flip Over window in its path.

Notes is displayed on the right side of the display, while the Translate application is active on the left. The clock is displayed in a Flip Over box that partially obscures Notes.

INITIATE APP SWITCHING USING SLIDE-OVER

Tap and hold the bottom part of the Move Over the window or perform one of the subsequent actions:

❖ From the bottom of your Slide Over window, swipe halfway across the screen, hesitate, and then raise your finger.
 Each Slide Over window becomes visible.
❖ Tap the application that is visible and that you wish to examine.
 Swipe both ways when it is not visible to navigate through the applications

Slide Over Windows launches four applications, namely Mail, pictures, Translate, and Notes.

In Slide Over, you can also utilize the App Switcher as a way to navigate between applications.

MODIFY THE SLIDE OVER INTERFACE

Perform one of the subsequent actions:

❖ To reposition the Slide Over program to the opposite side of the display, use the dragging function located above the Slide Over window's Multitasking Controls icon.

❖ To temporarily conceal the Slide Over the window swipe the Performing multiple tasks Controls icon, swipe all of the way towards the bottom of your Slide Over window, or drag the sides of the box to the left margin of the screen. A link appears in its place to signify that the Slide Over box remains accessible after it has vanished.

❖ To restore the Slide throughout the window to the screen, drag the icon denoting the window from the screen's left edge.

CONVERTING THE SLIDE OVER INTO A SPLIT VIEW

Press the Split Display button ⊞ after clicking the Performing Multiple Tasks Controls button ••• located at the very top of the Flip Over window. To move the current application to the left-hand side of the display, select the Left Splitting View button ▣. Alternatively, to move it to the right side, select the Right Splitting View button ▣.

LAUNCH AN ITEM LOCATED IN THE SCREEN'S CENTRE

In numerous iPad applications, such as Mail, messaging, Notes, and Files, an item can be accessed from the app window's center.

❖ Perform one of the following:
  ✓ In Mail, you can touch and retain any message in a mailbox.
  ✓ Maintain a conversation through touch in Messages.
  ✓ In Notes, touch and retain a note.
❖ Select the Opening in New Window option.
  The item appears in the center of the screen, directly above the current view, without causing any other modifications to the screen layout.

Tip: Additionally, every one of the items enumerated in Step 1 can be accessed in another window in the screen's center by pinch-opening them.

By touching the corresponding buttons, you can convert a center window to full screen, split view, or slide over. To switch a center window to a split view, press the Split View button. To switch to a slide-over, tap the Slide Over icon.

VIEW THE OPEN WINDOWS AS WELL AS WORKSPACES OF AN APPLICATION

Several iPad applications, including Mail, Notebooks, Safari, and Files, permit the operation of numerous windows simultaneously. All current windows for an application are visible, including those in Slide Over and Split View.

UNLOCK THE WINDOWS OF AN APPLICATION

- ❖ Perform one of the following:
  - ✓ Swipe upward from the screen's bottom margin to access the dock.
  - ✓ Access the Home interface.
- ❖ Hold the application whose windows you wish to display in your hand, and then press Show All Windows.

  Please be advised that prolonged touch-and-hold interactions with an app will cause all of the applications to commence jiggling. Try again after tapping Done or pressing the Home icon (on an iPad using the Home button).

Certain applications display active windows as thumbnails located in the lower portion of the display. The contents of a thumbnail are displayed in the current large in-size window when it is tapped. To view all open windows of an application while using Split View, select the Multitasking Controls icon located at the top of the app.

CREATING FRESH WINDOWS WITHIN AN APPLICATION

You observe the New Window icon ✛ when all of the open windows of an application appear as icons (near the bottom of the screen). To launch the application in a new window, tap it. To display the app's window open as thumbnails in Split View, select the Multitasking Control button ··· followed by the New Window button ✛.

ORGANIZE, RESIZE, AND RELOCATE WINDOWS ON IPAD USING STAGE MANAGER

On models that are supported, Stage Manager is an innovative method to multitask and complete tasks efficiently. You can adjust the dimensions of windows to your liking, view multiple windows that overlap in one view, and transition between applications by tapping.

Grouping applications for particular projects or duties enables you to reorganize, overlap, and resize them to achieve the desired layout.

When an iPad is linked to an exterior display, Stage Manager can be utilized to manipulate windows by dragging them between the iPad and the external display to achieve the desired arrangement.

TOGGLE STAGE MANAGER BETWEEN ON AND OFF

When Stage Manager is activated, the active application resides in the center of the screen at a scale that facilitates manipulation. A listing of recent applications appears along the right side of the display as all other open applications transition to the left.

A display on an iPad with Stage Manager active. Other recently launched applications are listed on the screen's left-hand side, with the current window positioned in the center.

❖ Navigate to Settings ⚙ > Gestures & Multitasking.

❖ Tap the checkbox next to Stage Manager to enable Recent Applications.

Alternatively, Stage Manager can be accessed by launching Control Centre and selecting the Stage Manager option ⬚ .

UTILIZE MULTIPLE WINDOWS TO MULTITASK

You can group applications in Stage Manager for particular duties or projects and maintain their group status. Windows may be resized, repositioned, and overlapped per the workflow.

❖ To group an application with the one you are currently using, perform one of the following:

✓ At the top of a window, press the Multitasking Controls icon, then select Add Another Window. The current windows are displaced to display the windows of all recent applications. Tap the item to add it.

✓ By touching and holding an application from the Recent Programs list, it can be dragged to the center of the screen to the present window.

✓ By touching and holding an application in the Dock, it can be dragged to the screen's center.
(To disclose the Dock, swipe up just far enough from the bottom margin of the display if it is not already visible.)

✓ By selecting the Application Library icon (located at the rightmost position in the Dock), select an app icon, and then hold it in your hand while dragging it to the center of the display.

The iPad display was activated with Stage Manager. Other recent applications are listed in a column to the left of the screen, while three current frames are grouped in the center. The Dock applications are displayed at the bottom of the display.

❖ While utilizing multiple applications, perform any of the following:
- ✓ To resize a window, use the trackpad or mouse to drag from any point or boundary of the window, or the corner indicated with a dark curve.
- ✓ To add a window to the most recent application list, select Minimize from the Multitasking Controls menu at the top of the window.
- ✓ Drag a window by doing so from its uppermost corner.
- ✓ To enlarge a window, select Enter Full Screen from the Multitasking Controls icon located at the top of the window.

Tip: On supported models, to obtain additional workspace, navigate to Settings > Display and Brightness, select Display Zoom, and then More Space. Implementing this setting enables you to observe a greater amount of content in your applications while working in multiple tabs via Split-Over or Stage Manager.

HOW TO TOGGLE BETWEEN APPLICATIONS

In Stage Manager, app switching is accomplished by selecting a symbol in the Dock or another application from the Recent apps list.

The application or group in which you were working is relocated to the Recent applications list to the left and substituted with the one that was touched upon.

Additionally, one of the following can be used to swap apps:

❖ To view recently added applications and groups, swipe upwards from the bottom of the display and pause in the center.
❖ Utilize one finger to swipe either left or right along the bottom perimeter of the display. (If your iPad has a Home icon, execute this action by tracing a faint arc.)
❖ Four to five digits should be used to swipe to the left or right.

DISPLAY OR CONCEAL THE RECENT APPLICATIONS LIST

Perform one of the subsequent actions:

❖ Tap as well as hold the Scene Manager icon ⬜ in the Control Centre before selecting the checkbox to the left of the image.

❖ Select Recent Apps by navigating to Settings ⚙ > Multitasking and Gestures and tapping the checkbox next to Stage Manager to enable or disable it.

An iPad display containing the buttons for activating or deactivating Stage Manager, concealing or displaying the inventory of recently installed applications, and hiding or activating the Dock.

If the recent applications list automatically conceals when a window is moved too near to it, sliding from the left margin of the screen will cause it to reappear.

EXIT A WINDOW

Select Close by tapping the Multitasking Controls icon
• • • at the top of the window.

If a window is contained within an application group, it is removed from the group.

TRANSFER A PROGRAM TO AN EXTERNAL MONITOR

You can work throughout both screens if your iPad (models supported) is linked to an external display; simply drag and drop applications and the windows between the two displays to organize them as you see fit.

To relocate applications between displays, perform one of the subsequent:

❖ You can transition the application window from a single display to another by dragging it from its top.
❖ Select the application whose icon you wish to relocate and drag it.

UTILIZE FUNCTIONS VIA THE LOCK SCREEN

When the iPad is powered on or awoke, the Lock Screen is displayed, encompassing the most recent notifications and the date and time at the moment. You can access notifications, the Camera, and the Control Centre, as well as information from your preferred applications, all from the Lock Screen.

By selecting a wallpaper, displaying a preferred photo, altering the font size of the time, inserting widgets, and doing so, you can customize your Lock Screen.

The left-hand side of the iPad security screen displays the time, date, and applications

INITIATE OPERATIONS AND ACCESS INFORMATION FROM THE DISPLAY WHILE LOCKED

The Lock Screen provides fast access to the most important information and features, even when the iPad is in a locked state.

❖ To activate the camera, swipe left.

❖ Slide down from the upper-right quadrant to access the Control Centre.

❖ To view notifications from the past, slide up from the center.

❖ For additional widgets, swipe right. On the Lock Screen and Home Screen, you may interact with widgets to accomplish tasks; for instance, to mark off an item in the Alerts widget, tap it, or to play an episode of Podcasts, touch the Play icon in the widget.

❖ To begin sketching and taking notes, select Apple Pencil from the Lock Screen (on supported models). In Notes, everything you create is saved.

❖ Utilize the playback controls (Currently Playing) located on the Lock Screen to operate the media player on your iPad. This includes the ability to play, pause, go back, or fast-forward.

Consult the Control access to data on the iPad security screen guide for details on how to modify the Lock Screen's content.

DISPLAY PREVIEWS OF NOTIFICATIONS ON THE LOCK SCREEN

❖ Navigate to the Settings > Notifications page.
❖ Followed by Show Previews, select Always.

Notification previews comprise information regarding Calendar invitations, text from Messages, and lines from Mail messages.

LIVE ACTIVITY VISIBILITY AND MANAGEMENT ON THE LOCKED SCREEN

Live Activities, such as order updates, deadlines, flight tracking, media playback, and live sports updates, are accessible from your Lock Screen, allowing you to follow along directly on your device.

A Live Activity on the iPad Lock Screen—an airline flight tracker that displays the expected departure time and time for the aircraft being monitored.

When playing music, a film, or any other content on the iPad, you can play, pause, resume, and fast-forward using the playback settings in Now Watching on the Lock Screen.

Additionally, media playback on an external device (such as a HomePod or Apple TV) can be managed from the iPad Lock Screen.

EXECUTE RAPID OPERATIONS ON THE IPAD

In applications, the Home Screen, Control Centre, and preview screens all provide access to fast action menus and additional functionality.

❖ Press and hold a picture in Photos to examine a preview and a selection of available options.
❖ By touching and holding the message in an inbox in Mail, one can access a selection of options and a preview of the message's contents.

- ❖ To access a fast actions menu, press and hold the application icon momentarily on the Home Screen. Tap Done in the upper-right corner or select the Home icon (on an iPad using the Home button) if the icons begin to vibrate, and then attempt again.
- ❖ To access options, launch Control Centre, then contact and hold an item such as the brightness control or the camera.
- ❖ To respond to a notification displayed on the locked screen, momentarily touch and hold it.
- ❖ Hold down the Space bar using one finger while typing to transform the on-screen keyboard onto a trackpad.

USE SPOTLIGHT TO SEARCH ON AN IPAD

With an iPad, you can use Live Text to look for text in your photographs as well as applications, contacts, and content within applications like Mail and Messages. In addition to finding and opening websites, applications, and photographs in your photo collection, across the system and online, you can also check stock & currency information.

App shortcuts for what you'll probably do next when you browse for an app show up in the Top Hit. (For instance, when you browse for Photos, a direct link to the Favourites album displays.)

With the iPad, you can conduct searches from anywhere, including the lock screen, and choose what applications to show up in the search results. As you write, Search changes its results and makes recommendations depending on how you use the app.

SELECT WHICH APPLICATIONS TO ADD TO THE SEARCH

❖ Navigate to Siri & Search in Settings⚙.
❖ Scroll down, touch an app, and choose whether to enable or disable Show App in Search.

UTILIZE THE IPAD TO SEARCH

❖ From either the Lock Screen or the Home Screen, swipe down.
❖ Type your search term into the search box.
❖ Take one of the following actions:
   ✓ Start your search by tapping Search or Proceed.
   ✓ Launch the recommended app: Press the application.
   ✓ Act immediately: You may run any shortcut, set a timer, activate Focus, use Shazam to determine the title of a song and much more. Use the Shortcuts app to build your shortcuts, or search for the name of an app to discover what shortcuts are available.
   ✓ Visit this recommended website: Press it.
   ✓ Find out more details about the suggested search: To open it, touch it and then one of the results.
   ✓ Launch a fresh search: In the search area, click the Clear Text option ⊗.

DISABLE LOCATION-BASED RECOMMENDATIONS

❖ Navigate to Location Services under Settings > Privacy & Security.
❖ After selecting System Services, disable Suggestions & Search

SEARCH THROUGH THE APPLICATIONS

Many applications provide a search function or button that lets you look for content within the program. For instance, you may look for a certain area using the Maps app.

❖ Press the search area or the button $\mathcal{Q}$ for Search (if available) in an app.
Swipe downward from the top if there isn't a button or search box visible.
❖ After typing in your query, hit Search.

INCLUDE A DICTIONARY

You may install dictionaries on your iPad so that you can utilize them for searches.

❖ Select General > Dictionary under Settings.
❖ Pick out a dictionary.

VIEWING OR MODIFYING CELLULAR DATA SETTINGS (WI-FI PLUS CELLULAR MODELS)

On the iPad, you can choose which applications and services utilize cellular data as well as enable and deactivate cellular data access. It is also possible to switch up your data package with certain providers.

5G networks may be connected to compatible models.

Note: Get in touch with your wireless network provider for assistance with billing and cellular network services.

A symbol denoting the cellular network displays in the status bar if the iPad is linked to the internet via the cellular data network.

All data services, including web surfing, email, and push notifications, rely only on Wi-Fi when cellular data is turned off. Carriers may charge you if your cell data is enabled. For instance, utilizing certain data-transfer features and services, like Messages, may result in costs to your data plan.

Note: Wi-Fi + Cellular versions only offer cellular data transfer; they do not support cellular phone service. Use Wi-Fi Calling with an iPhone to place calls from an iPad.

UPGRADE YOUR IPAD WITH A CELLULAR PLAN

If you've already configured a cellular schedule, go to Setting ⚙ > Cellular, choose Add a Newer Plan, and then adhere to the prompts on the screen.

ACCESS OR MODIFY YOUR MOBILE DATA ACCOUNT

Navigate to Settings 🌐 > Cellular Data and choose Carrier Services or Manage [account name].

SELECT CELLULAR DATA PLANS BASED ON PERFORMANCE, BATTERY LIFE, DATA USE, AND OTHER FACTORS

Navigate to Settings 🌐 > Cellular to enable or disable Cellular Data.

Go to Settings> Cellular > Mobile Data settings, then choose one of the following actions to configure settings when Mobile Data is enabled:

❖ Cut down on mobile phone use by turning on Low Information Mode, or depending on the model of your iPad, by tapping Data Mode and selecting Low Data Mode. When the iPad is not linked to Wi-Fi, this mode stops background operations and automatic upgrades.
❖ Turn on or off data roaming: When you're in an area that isn't serviced by your carrier's network, data roaming enables you to access the internet via a cellular data network. You may prevent roaming fees while traveling by disabling data roaming.

The following option could be accessible to you, depending on the model, carrier, and area of your iPad:

❖ Activate or deactivate LTE: Activating LTE speeds up data loading.

The following functions are available on the iPad Pro 12.9-square inch (5th version) and ipads Pro 11-inch (3rd version) (Wi-Fi + Cellular):

❖ To maximize battery life, turn on Smart Data mode: Select 5G Auto after tapping Voice & Data. When 5G speeds don't significantly outperform LTE in this mode, the iPad will automatically switch to LTE.
❖ Utilize FaceTime HD and higher-quality video on 5G networks: Select Allow additional data on 5G after tapping Data Mode.

TO START SHARING THE IPAD'S CELLULAR INTERNET CONNECTION, SET UP A PERSONAL HOTSPOT

❖ Turn on Mobile Data by going to Settings 🌐 > Cellular.
❖ After selecting Create Personal Hotspot, according to the guidelines provided in Sharing your iPad's Internet Connection (Wi-Fi + Cellular).

LIMIT THE USAGE OF CELLULAR DATA FOR SERVICES AND APPLICATIONS

Toggling Mobile Data off or on for any application (like Maps) or service (like Wi-Fi Assist) that utilizes cellular data requires going to Settings 🌐 > Cellular Data.

iPad only makes use of Wi-Fi when a setting is off.

Note: By default, Wi-Fi Assist is on. Wi-Fi Assistance turns to mobile data to strengthen the signal if the Wi-Fi connection is low. When you have a bad Wi-Fi connection, you continue to utilize cellular data to access the internet, which might result in extra costs based on your data plan.

SECURE YOUR SIM CARD

You may prevent unauthorized users from using your SIM card by using a personal identifying number (PIN) to lock it if your device needs one for cellular data. Following that, every time you reboot your device and replace the SIM card, the card locks by itself, and you're forced to enter the PIN number.

CHAPTER THREE

CUSTOMIZE IPAD

HOW TO TURN OFF OR ADJUST THE SOUND

In Settings⚙, alter or turn off the noises the iPad plays whenever you receive a call, email, text message, reminder, or other sort of notification.

To temporarily quiet incoming calls, notifications, and sound effects, switch on Do Not Disturb.

Set sound choices

Set choices for alert tones & ringtones, & ringer, and alert loudness.

* ❖ Navigate to Sounds under Settings.
* ❖ To adjust the ringer and notification volume, drag the slider.
* ❖ To choose sounds for the alert tones and ringtone, click Ringtone and other choices.

The noises that the iPad plays for some people may also be altered. Navigate to Contacts⚙, choose the contact's name, select Edit, and then select a text and ringtone.

SILENCING THE IPAD

To turn off sound effects, alarms, and incoming calls temporarily, open Control Centre, choose Focus, and then select Do Not Disturb.

Tip: Open Control Centre and make sure Do Not Disturb is turned on if you're not getting incoming calls or alerts when you should. Should the "Do Not Disturb" button be highlighted, just press it to disable the feature. (The Do Not Disturb symbol may be shown in the status bars when it is enabled.)

MAKE A PERSONALIZED IPAD LOCK SCREEN

Choose a wallpaper, show off a favorite picture, alter the clock font, add widgets, and do a lot more to customize your lock screen.

It is possible to create many Lock Screens, toggling between them, and even connecting a security screen to a Concentration. Thus, you may designate a certain Lock Screen for use when working, for instance.

CUSTOMIZE A FRESH LOCK SCREEN

❖ To add a new button🟢, hover over the Lock button until the Customize option appears at the bottom of the screen.
Press and hold the security screen once again, then input your passcode, if they aren't visible.

❖ To add a new lock display, hit the Add New button🟢
. To edit an existing lock screen, slide to the desired area of the screen, select Customize, and then click Lock Screen.

The Add Fresh Wallpaper screen offers a selection of wallpaper options organized into categories like Featured & Suggested Photos for personalizing the iPhone Lock Screen. The buttons to add images, people, emoticons, a photo shuffle, and a weather display backdrop to the Lock Screen are located at the top.

❖ Click one of your wallpaper choices to set it as the lock screen if you're making a new one.
Customize the lock screen picture if you select Photos or Picture Shuffle.

❖ To alter the font, color, and style, tap the time.
To adjust the font's weight, drag the slider (that is accessible for solid fonts only).

❖ Click Add Widget or the date to add widgets containing data like the current headlines, the current climate, and upcoming events on the calendar. To add widgets to the left-hand side of the display while the device is in landscape mode, hit the Add Widgets button on the left. Under the time, choose Add Widgets in portrait mode. You may also put widgets atop the time.

A personalized lock screen that is being modified. The day of the week, the time, & a button to add widgets are the elements that may be customized.

❖ Select Add or Done, then choose Customize Home Screen or Set as Wallpaper Pair.

    ✓ *Select whether you want the wallpaper to appear on the home screen as well as the lock screen*: Select "Set as Wallpaper Pair."

    ✓ *Make more adjustments to the Main Screen*: Select the Customize Home Screen option. You may use a personalized picture by tapping the Pictures button ; alter the wallpaper color by tapping a color; or blur the background to make the applications stand out by selecting Blur.

An image of the Earth fills the iPad lock screen. Widgets for the weather, Apple Pencil batteries, a clock, a calendar, and reminders are located on the left side.

PERSONALIZE THE PICTURE ON YOUR LOCK SCREEN

You may adjust the photo's location, style, and other aspects if you choose it to be your lock screen image.

Take one of the following actions:

❖ *Reposition your photo*: Pinch open to zoom in on the chosen picture, drag with your fingers to rotate it, then squeeze closed to zoom out to change its position.

❖ *Modify the style of the photo*: To experiment with several picture styles using complimentary color filters and typefaces, swipe left or right.

❖ *Multilayered effect creation*: To create a multilayered effect, choose Depth Effect from the menu by tapping the More button located at the bottom right of the image, if it allows layering, such as a picture of people, pets, or the sky.

Note: On supported models, the multilayer effect is accessible. If the topic is too excessive or low, or when it covers up excessive amounts of the clock, layering might not be possible.

❖ *Use a Live Photo to create a motion effect*: If you choose a Live Picture that can be slowed down, you may play it when the gadget wakes up by tapping the Play button ▶ located at the bottom left of the screen.

❖ *Adjust the shuffle regularity*: If you pick Picture Shuffle ⊞, you can use the Browse button to get a sample of the photographs and the More button to select an option underneath Shuffle Frequency to adjust the shuffle frequency.

As an alternative, you may directly add a picture to your Lock Screen and Home Screen from your photo library. Select a picture by tapping Library in the Photos app 🌸, and then hit the Share button ⬆. Choose Use as Wallpaper by swiping down, tapping Add, and then selecting whether to have it appear on your lock screen and home screen.

MAKE A FOCUS PART OF YOUR LOCK SCREEN

Focus reduces outside distractions so you can focus on the job at hand. You may configure a Focus to either enable just specified alerts (those relevant to your job, for example) or to temporarily disable all notifications.

When you associate a Focus with a Lock Screen, the Focus's preferences are used each time you access that specific Lock Screen.

* Once the Customize button shows at the bottom of your screen, touch and grasp the Lock Screen.
* To view the Focus choices, such as Not to Disturb, Personal, Rest, and Work, tap Focus toward the bottom of your wallpaper.
* After choosing a Focus, press the Close button.

MODIFY OR ALTER YOUR LOCK SCREEN

You may make modifications to your personalized Lock Screen after you've created it.

* To add a new button, hold down the Lock Screen icon until the Customize option appears at the bottom of the screen.
  Press and hold the security screen once again, then input your passcode, if they aren't visible.
* To make changes, swipe to the desired screen, choose Customize, and then select Lock Screen.
* To alter the font, color, and style, tap the time.
* Tap Add Widget or the date to add widgets containing data like the current headlines, the climate, and upcoming events on the calendar.
* Select Add or Done, then choose Customize Home Screen or Set as Wallpaper Pair.

TOGGLE BETWEEN THE LOCK SCREENS

It is possible to make many personalized lock screens and alternate between them over the day.

❖ Once the Customize button shows at the bottom of your screen, press and hold it to activate the Lock Screen.
❖ Select the Lock Screen by swiping on it, and then tapping it.
It should be noted that if your Lock Screen ties to a certain Focus, changing Lock Screens will also change your Focus. See Attach a Lock Screen to a Focus.

ELIMINATE A LOCK SCREEN

Lock Screens that are no longer needed may be removed.

❖ Once the Customize button shows at the bottom of the screen, hover over it to activate the Lock Screen.
❖ To erase a lock screen, slide to go to it, then swipe up to reveal the Trash button.

Tip: You can programmatically change your Lock Screen by first connecting it to a Focus and then automatically changing to that specific Focus.

MODIFYING THE IPAD'S WALLPAPER

Select a picture or photo to use as your iPad's home screen or lock screen wallpaper. Both static and dynamic picture options are available.

The Wallpaper Setting screen displays pictures of your Lock Screen & the main screen with the selected wallpaper at the very top along with a button for selecting a new wallpaper.

ALTER THE WALLPAPER

❖ Select Add New Wallpaper under Settings > Wallpaper.

The collection of wallpapers opens.

❖ Take one of the following actions:

✓ To customize your wallpaper with an image, an emoji pattern, an image of the weather where you live, and more, tap one of the buttons at the very top of your wallpaper gallery, such as pictures, Photo Motion Live Photo, & so on.

✓ Select a wallpaper from any of the highlighted collections (weather, astronomy, collections, etc.).

- ❖ See Customize the Lock Screen picture to make changes to your photo if you're adding a picture or Photo Slide to the background.
- ❖ After selecting one of the options below, tap Add.
  - ✓ Designated as a Pair of Wallpapers
  - ✓ Personalize Your Home Screen

MAKE A PERSONALIZED IPAD LOCK SCREEN

Choose a wallpaper, show off a favorite picture, alter the clock font, add widgets, and do a lot more to customize your lock screen.

It is possible to create many Lock Screens, toggling between them, and even connecting an encrypted screen to a Concentration. Thus, you may designate a certain Lock Screen for use when working, for instance.

Customize a fresh lock screen

- ❖ To add a new button⊕, hover over the Lock Screen icon until the Customize option appears at the bottom of the screen.
  Press and hold the security screen once again, then input your passcode, if they aren't visible.
- ❖ To add a new lock display, hit the Add New button ⊕. To edit an existing lock screen, slide to the desired area of the screen, select Customize, and then click Lock Screen.

The Add New Background screen offers a selection of wallpaper options organized into categories like Featured & Suggested Photos for personalizing the iPhone Lock Screen. The buttons to add images, people, emoticons, a photo shuffle, and a weather display backdrop to the Lock Screen are located at the top.

❖ Click one of the image choices to set it as the lock screen if you're making a new one.
Customize the lock screen picture if you select Photos or Picture Shuffle.

❖ To alter the color, font, and style, tap the time.
To adjust the font's weight, drag the slider (that is accessible for solid fonts only).

❖ Click Add Widgets and the date to add widgets containing data like the current headlines, the climate, and upcoming events on the calendar. To add widgets to the left side of the screen while the device is in landscape mode, hit the Add Widgets button on the left. Under the time, choose Add Widgets in portrait mode. Widgets may be added above the time as well.

A personalized lock screen that is being modified. The date, time, & a button to add widgets are the elements that may be customized.

❖ Select Add or Done, then choose Customize Home Screen or Set as Wallpaper Pair.
  ✓ Select whether you want the wallpaper to appear on the home screen as well as the lock screen: Select "Set as Wallpaper Pair."
  ✓ Make more adjustments to the Home Display: Select the Customize Home Screen option. You may use a personalized picture by tapping the picture On the Rectangle button, alter the wallpaper color by tapping a color, or blur the background to make the applications stand out by selecting Blur.

An image of the Earth fills the iPad lock screen. Widgets for the weather, Apple Pencil batteries, a clock, a calendar, and reminders are located on the left side.

PERSONALIZE THE PICTURE ON YOUR LOCK SCREEN

You may adjust the photo's location, style, and other aspects if you choose it to be your lock screen image.

Take one of the following actions:

❖ Reposition your photo: Pinch open to zoom in on the chosen picture, drag with a pair of fingers to move it, and afterward, pinch shut to zoom out to change its position.

❖ Modify the style of the photo: To experiment with several picture styles using complimentary color filters and typefaces, swipe left or right.

❖ To create a multilayered effect, choose Depth Effect from the menu by tapping the More button located at the bottom right of the image, if it allows layering, such as a picture of people, pets, or the sky.

Note: On supported models, the multilayer effect is accessible. If the topic is too excessive or low, or when it covers up an excessive amount of the clock, layering might not be possible.

❖ Use a Live Photo to create a motion effect. If you choose a Live Picture that can be slowed down, you may play it when the gadget wakes up by tapping the Play button located in the bottom left of the screen.

❖ Adjust the shuffle regularity: If you pick Photo Shuffle, then can use the Browse button to get a sample of the photographs and the More button to select an option underneath Shuffle Frequency to adjust the shuffle frequency.

As an alternative, you may directly add a picture to your Lock Screen and Home Screen from your photo library. Select a picture by tapping Library in the Photos app, and then hit the Share button. Choose Use as Wallpaper by swiping down, tapping Add, and then selecting whether to have it appear on your lock screen and home screen.

MAKE A FOCUS PART OF YOUR LOCK SCREEN

Focus reduces outside distractions so you can focus on the job at hand. You may configure a Focus to either enable just specified alerts (those relevant to your job, for example) or to temporarily disable all notifications. When you associate a Focus with a Lock Screen, your Focus's preferences are used each time you access that specific Lock Screen.

❖ Once the Customize button shows at the bottom of your screen, press and hold it to activate the Lock Screen.

❖ To view the Focus choices, such as Never Disturb, Personal, Rest, and Work, tap Focus toward the bottom of the wallpaper.

❖ After choosing a Focus, press the Close button.

MODIFY OR ALTER YOUR LOCK SCREEN

You may make modifications to your personalized Lock Screen after you've created it.

❖ To add a new button ⊕, hover over the locked screen until the Customize option appears at the bottom of the screen.
Press and hold the security screen once again, then input your passcode, if they aren't visible.

❖ To make changes, swipe to the desired screen, choose Customize, and then select Lock Screen.

❖ To alter the font, color, and style, tap the time.

❖ Tap Add Widget or the date to add widgets containing data like the current headlines, the climate, and upcoming events on the calendar.

❖ Select Add or Done, then choose Customize Home Screen or Set as Wallpaper Pair.

TOGGLE BETWEEN THE LOCK SCREENS

It is possible to make many personalized lock screens and alternate between them over the day.

❖ Once the Customize button shows at the bottom of your screen, hover over it to activate the Lock Screen.

❖ Select the Lock Screen by swiping on it, and then tapping it.
It should be noted that if a screen's lock ties to a certain Focus, changing Lock Screens will also change your Focus.

ELIMINATE A LOCK SCREEN

Lock Screens that are no longer needed may be removed.

❖ Once the Customize button shows at the bottom of your screen, press and hold it to activate the Lock Screen.

❖ To erase a lock screen, slide to go to it, then swipe up to reveal the Trash button 🗑.

CHANGE THE SCREEN'S COLOUR AND BRIGHTNESS

You may adjust the brightness and dimmer of your iPad screen (dimming the screen prolongs battery life). Additionally, you may use Dark Mode, True Colour, and Night Shift to manually or automatically change the brightness and color of the screen.

MANUALLY ADJUST THE SCREEN'S BRIGHTNESS

Any of the following actions will adjust the brightness or dimmer of your iPad screen:

❖ To adjust the brightness bar, open Control Centre and drag it (the brightness bar ☀) down or up.
❖ Drag the slider after selecting Display & Brightness under Settings.

AUTOMATICALLY ADJUST THE SCREEN'S BRIGHTNESS

The iPad's built-in ambient light sensor is used to automatically adapt the screen brightness to the current lighting conditions.

❖ Navigate to Accessibility under Settings⚙.
❖ After selecting Display and Text Size, activate Auto-Brightness.

TURN THE DARK MODE ON OR OFF

The iPad's whole experience is given a dark color palette via Dark Mode, which is ideal for dimly lit areas. You may use your iPad in Dark Mode to read in bed, for example, without bothering the person sitting next to you.

Take one of the following actions:

- ❖ To enable or disable Dark Mode, open Control Centre, press and hold the Lightness button ☀, then hit the Appearance button ◐.
- ❖ To activate Dark Mode, go to Settings ⚙ > Display & Brightness; to deactivate it, choose Light.

The home screen of the iPad in dark mode

SET UP AN AUTOMATED SCHEDULE FOR DARK MODE TO SWITCH ON AND OFF

In Settings, you may program Dark Mode to activate immediately at night (or according to a certain time).

- ❖ Navigate to Display & Brightness under Settings ⚙.
- ❖ Select Options after turning on Automatic.
- ❖ Choose Custom Schedule or Sunset to Sunrise.
  If you select Custom Schedule, you may arrange the times when Dark Mode will switch on and off by tapping the available choices.

When you choose Sunset to Sunrise, your iPad determines when it is evening for you based on your geolocation and clock data.

TURN ON OR OFF THE NIGHT SHIFT

Night Shift may be manually activated, which is useful if you find yourself in a dimly lit environment during the day.

To activate the Night Shift button, open Control Centre, touch and hold the Lightness button.

SET UP THE NIGHT SHIFT TO SWITCH ON AND OFF ON ITS OWN

To make seeing the screen simpler on your eyes at night, schedule Night Shift, which will move the display's colors to the warmer side of the color spectrum.

❖ Navigate to Display and Brightness > Settings 🛞 > Night Shift.
❖ Activate Scheduled.
❖ Drag the slider under Colour Temperature to the warmer or colder end of the spectrum to change the color balance for Night Shift.
❖ Choose Custom Schedule or Sunset to Sunrise after tapping From.
   If you select Custom Schedule, you can set the times that you want the night shift to be turned on and off by tapping the available choices.

When you choose Sunset to Sunrise, your iPad determines when it is evening for you based on your geolocation and clock data.

Note: If you disabled Location Services under Settings > Security and Privacy or Setting Time Zone under Settings ⚙ > Privacy and Security > Location Accounts > System Services, you will not be able to use the Sunset till Sunrise option.

MAKE THE IPAD SCREEN LARGER BY USING DISPLAY ZOOM

With the iPad Pro 12.9-inch, users may use Display Zoom to enlarge the screen.

❖ Navigate to Display & Brightness under Settings ⚙.
❖ Select Show Zoom and then Select Larger Text.
❖ Once Done, choose Use Zoomed.

MODIFY THE TIME AND DATE

Depending on where you are, the Lock Screen's date and time are automatically updated. You may modify them if you'd like—for instance, while you're on the road.

❖ Navigate to Date & Time under Settings ⚙ > General.
❖ Activate one or both of the following:
    ✓ **Set Automatically:** Your iPad adjusts its time to reflect your current time zone by obtaining the accurate time via the network. The iPad may not

be capable of automatically detecting the local time in certain countries or areas because some networks do not support network time.

✓ **Twenty-four hours:** (not accessible in all areas or countries) The hours are shown on an iPad from zero to 23.

Turn off Set Manually and adjust the displayed date and time to replace the default ones.

ARRANGE YOUR APPLICATIONS INTO FOLDERS

To make your applications simpler to discover on the main screen pages, you may arrange them into folders.

CREATING A FOLDER

❖ Select Edit Home Screen after touching and holding any application on the Home Screen.
The applications start to shake.

❖ You may drag one app on top of another to form a folder.

❖ Other programs may be dragged inside the folder.
The folder may include many pages with programs on them.

❖ To change the folder's name, touch and grasp it, choose Rename, then type a new one.
Try again after tapping the backdrop of the Home Screen if the applications start to vibrate.

❖ Press Done once you're done.

Drag all the applications out of a folder after opening it with a touch to remove it. The folder is erased automatically.

It should be noted that how you arrange your applications on the main screen has no bearing on how they are arranged in the library of applications.

TRANSFER AN APP TO THE MAIN SCREEN FROM A FOLDER

To make an app simpler to locate and launch, you may move it from the folder to a page on your home screen.

❖ Navigate to the app's folder on the Home Screen page, then press the folder to launch it.
❖ After you touch and hold an app, it will start to jitter.
❖ From the folder, drag the app to the Main Screen.

RETURN APPLICATIONS AND THE HOME SCREEN TO THEIR DEFAULT SETTINGS.

❖ Select Reset under Settings > General.
❖ Select Reset Layout of Home Screen.
   Applications that you have downloaded are arranged alphabetically after the applications that came with the device, and any folders you have established are erased.

ADD, MODIFY, AND DELETE WIDGETS

WIDGETS: WHAT ARE THEY?

With widgets, you can quickly access up-to-date information such as the headlines for the day, the weather, notifications, battery levels, & more. To have this information always at hand, you may add widgets to your main screen/Lock Screen and see them in Today View.

Without opening the app, you can communicate with widgets on the main screen and Lock Screen. You can do things with the widgets for Contacts, Music, Podcasts, Safari, and more. To play a selection, for instance, hit the play icon on the Podcasts or Music widget.

TO YOUR HOME SCREEN, ADD A WIDGET

❖ To add a widget, go to the desktop page you want it on, then tap and hold the backdrop of the Home Screen until the applications start to jiggle.

❖ To access the widget gallery, tap the Add Widgets button + located at the very top of the screen.

❖ Once you've found the widget you're looking for by scrolling or searching, press it, and then slide left and right to adjust the size.
Different information is shown by the various sizes.

❖ Click Add Widget after you've found the desired size.

❖ Move the widget to the desired location on the screen while the applications are still jiggling, then choose Done.

You can keep widgets on your Home Screen.

The iPad Home Screen. Customized widgets for the weather, music, pictures, reminders, and home are located at the very top of the screen.

A Smart Stack, shown by dots next to it, is a collection of widgets that automatically displays the most appropriate widget at the right time of day based on factors like the current time, location, and activity. A Smart Stack may be added to the Main Screen, and its widgets can be seen by swiping up or down through it.

INTERACTING WITH THE WIDGETS

Widgets on your Lock Screen or Home Screen may be used for tasks. Without opening an app, you can check off items in the Reminders widget, play an episode from the Podcasts widget by tapping the Play button, and switch on the lights in your living room by tapping the Home widget.

EDITING A WIDGET ON THE HOME SCREEN

Most widgets may be customized to provide the data you want to view directly from your Home Screen. For instance, you may change a weather widget to show the prediction for a different place or yourself. Alternatively, you may set up a Smart Stack to dynamically switch between its widgets according to your activity, where you are, what time of day it is, and other factors.

❖ To access the fast actions menu, just touch and hold any widget on your Home Screen.
❖ Select choices by tapping Edit Widget (or Edit Stack, if it's a Smart Stack).
   You may drag a widget from a Smart Stack to the Main Screen, enable or disable Widget Suggestions or Smart Rotate, and delete a widget by hitting the minus symbol (−) in the top-left corner.
   When you activate Widget Suggestions, based on your previous use, recommended widgets for applications you currently use will show up in the Smart Stack automatically at the appropriate moment. You may add a widget to the stack using an option so that it is always available when you require it.
❖ Click "Done."

WIDGET REMOVAL FROM THE HOME SCREEN

❖ Simply hold down the widget to bring up the quick actions box

❖ After selecting Remove Stack or Remove Widget, choose Remove.

UTILIZE AND PERSONALIZE IPAD CONTROL CENTRE

Instant access to helpful functions, including flight mode, Do Not Disturb, flashlight, audio volume, screen brightness, and applications, is provided via iPad Control Centre.

Touch and hold to see Camera options.

The iPad Control Center. In the Control Centre of Wi-Fi + Mobile iPad models, the controls for Bluetooth, Wi-Fi, cellular data, and airplane mode are located in the top-left group. At the bottom side is the camera control.

LAUNCHING THE CONTROL CENTRE

To shut it, swipe upward from the bottom; to open it, swipe downward toward the top-right corner.

EXPAND YOUR CONTROL CENTRE CONTROL OPTIONS

Numerous controls provide more choices. Press down on a control to view the available alternatives. In the Control Centre, for instance, you may do the following tasks:

❖ To access the AirDrop choices, press and hold the top-most set of controls, and then hit the AirDrop button.

❖ For taking a selfie, shooting a movie, snapping a picture, or shooting a slow-motion video, just hold down the Camera button.

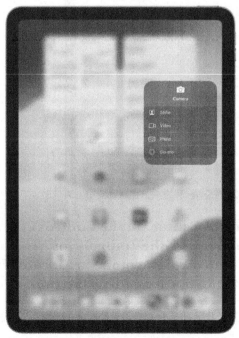

When you press and hold the camera's control, a screen displays the extra Camera settings that are accessible in the Control Centre. Selfie, Video, Picture, and Slo-mo are the available choices.

INCLUDE AND ARRANGE CONTROLS

❖ Open the Control Centre by going to Settings⚙.

❖ Tap the Insert menu button ⊕ or the Delete button ⊖ to add or delete controls.

❖ Touch the Reorder icon ≡ next to an icon and drag it to a different location to reorder it.

EXIT FROM A WI-FI CONNECTION FOR A SHORT WHILE.

To rejoin, just hit the Wi-Fi Connect button 📶 in the Control Centre once again.

Press and hold the Wi-Fi Switching button 📶 to see the title of the linked Wi-Fi network.

When you move or restart your iPad, recognized networks are automatically joined, and AirPlay and AirDrop continue to function since Wi-Fi isn't switched off when you exit from a network. Navigate to Settings > Wi-Fi to disable Wi-Fi. (Tap the Wi-Fi Switching button 📶 in the Control Centre to switch on Wi-Fi again.) See Select iPad setting for travel for instructions on turning on or off Wi-Fi in the Control Centre when in airplane mode.

DISCONNECT FROM DEVICES WITH BLUETOOTH FOR THE TIME BEING

To enable connections, press the Bluetooth Switching button ⚡ in the Control Centre once more.

When you cut off from a device, Bluetooth® remains active, allowing for continued location accuracy & other services. Navigate to Settings > Bluetooth, select it, and then click the off button. In the Control Centre, press the Bluetooth Switching button ⚡ to reactivate Bluetooth.

DISABLE APP ACCESS TO CONTROL CENTRE

After selecting Settings ⚙ > Control Centre, disable Access Within Apps.

HOW TO VIEW AND REPLY NOTIFICATIONS

Notifications aid in staying updated; they inform you when an event has been rescheduled if you skipped a call, and more. You can personalize your alerts to display just the content that matters to you.

Note: You may be prompted by an app while using it to choose whether you wish to get alerts instantly, never, or as part of a scheduled summary. Later on, under Settings > Notifications, you may modify this option.

GO TO THE NOTIFICATION CENTRE TO FIND YOUR ALERTS

iPad shows alerts as they come unless you have disabled them with Focus and Do Not Disturb. You may check them later if you don't read them straight away since they are preserved in the Notification Centre.

You may do any of these actions to see the messages you receive in the Notification Centre:

❖ Swipe upwards toward the center of the screen to access the lock screen.
❖ Swipe toward the top center on other displays. If you have any previous alerts, you may see them by scrolling up.

Press the Home key (on compatible models) or swipe upwards from the bottom using one finger to exit the Notification Centre.

REPLYING NOTIFICATIONS

It's simpler to read and handle many alerts when they're grouped by app in the Notification Centre or displayed on the Lock Screen. Certain applications can organize their notifications based on attributes like subject or thread. Notifications that have been grouped show shown as little stacks, with your most recent notice at the top.

Take one of the following actions:

✓ To see individual alerts in a group, expand the group: Give the group a tap. Tap Show Less to end the group.

✓ To see a notice and take immediate action, if the application provides it: Grab and manipulate the alert.

✓ To launch the app for a notification: After tapping the alert, choose Open.

✓ To reply to a message when the iPad is locked: Grab and manipulate the alert.

PLAN A SUMMARY OF THE NOTICE

By setting up notifications to be sent as a summary, you may minimize the amount of distractions in your day. You can choose which alerts you want to include in the overview and when to get it.

With your most relevant alerts at the top, the notification overview is automatically arranged by priority depending on the present activity and is tailored just for you. Because the summary lets you interact with alerts at your own pace, it's quite helpful. By utilizing Focus to filter alerts while you're focused on an activity, you may extend this even further.

❖ To enable Scheduled Summary, go to Settings > Notification > Scheduled Summary.

❖ Decide which applications to include in your synopsis.

❖ Give your summary a time slot. To get an additional summary, choose Add Summary.

❖ Make sure the applications you choose to include in the summary are switched on by tapping the letters A through Z underneath applications in the Summary.

Note: You may need to enable notifications for an app if you wish to include it in your Notifications Summary but it doesn't show up in the A to Z list. Navigate to Settings > Alerts, select the application, and activate All Notifications.

CONFIGURE AN IPAD FOCUS

Focus is an attribute that reduces outside distractions to help you focus on a task. You may establish a Custom Focus or modify one of the pre-provided Focus choices, such as Work, Personal, or Sleep, to focus on a certain task. Focus may notify other people and applications that you're working and temporarily disable all notifications, or enable just certain notifications (those relevant to the task at hand, for example).

Similarly, you may personalize a Home Display page that features just Focus-related applications and set it as your Home Screen when you're focusing. Additionally, iPad recommends Home Screens including widgets and applications related to the Theme you are configuring.

A fast tip is to launch Control Centre, choose Focus, and then activate Do Not Disturb to immediately turn off all alerts.

ESTABLISH A FOCUS

You may choose which applications and users to get alerts from once you configure a Focus. You may, for instance, establish a Work Focused and restrict alerts to those from your colleagues and work-related applications.

❖ Navigate to Settings  > Focus and choose a focus (Personal, Sleep, or Work, for example).
  You may configure the settings listed in the procedure below for the selected Focus, but you are not required to set them up.

A screen displaying the six focus choices available: work, personal, sleep, drive, no messages while on the phone, and do not disturb. You may utilize the same Focused setting on all of your Apple devices if the Share Between Device option is enabled.

❖ You may choose which contacts and applications can give you alerts while you're focused. For a Focus, see Silence or accept alerts.

❖ Choose Options, then do one of the following actions:
  ✓ Silenced notifications may be seen in the Notification Centre or on the Lock Screen: Activate or deactivate Show On Lock Screen.
  ✓ During this Focus, dim the lock screen by turning on the dim lock screen.
  ✓ On Home Screen applications, hide the notification badges: Activate the notification badges that hide.
❖ Once you have chosen all of the choices, click the Back button ‹ located at the very top of the display.
❖ Touch the small Home Screen under Customize Screens, choose the screen, touch Done, and then click the Back button to select the Home Screen pages to use for this Focus.
❖ Turn on Access Across Devices (you have to be logged in with the same username and password on all of your devices) to share the Focus app across all of your Apple devices.

Once your Focus is configured, you can go back to Options > Focuses at any moment and modify any of the previously selected settings.

The Sleep Focus adheres to the Sleep schedule that you configure on your iPhone. Open the Health application on your iPhone, choose Browse, then Sleep to add or modify your sleep routine.

INCLUDE FOCUS FILTERS

You may apply app filters to a Focus setup to control what information applications display during the Focus. You may choose which calendar you'll be using during the Focus, for instance, or which mail account to utilize.

❖ Navigate to Options > Focus and choose the Focus to which you want to apply filters.
❖ (Below Focus Filters) Tap Add Filter.
❖ Select the data you'd like to see while the Focus by tapping an app, choosing it, and then tapping Continue.
  ✓ Calendar: Select the calendar that will be shown during the Focus.
  ✓ Mail: Select the accounts you'd like to use for mail during the Focus.
  ✓ Messages: Select the message discussions you'd like to see while in the Focus. For instance, you may choose to see just those from persons whose alerts you have consented to receive during this Focus.
  ✓ Safari: Select the Tab Group you'd like to work within the Focus.
❖ To add a filter to the Focus, tap Add.

ESTABLISH A PERSONALIZED FOCUS

You may build a Custom Focus if you'd like to focus on a task that isn't one of the available Focus choices.

❖ Go to Focus under Settings⚙.

❖ Select Custom after tapping the Add button 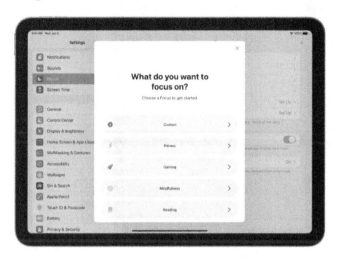 in the upper right corner.

An interface for configuring Focus on one of the other available choices, such as Custom, Fitness, Games, Mindfulness, and Reading

❖ After giving your Focus a name, hit Return.
❖ Select an icon and color to symbolize your Focus, then hit Next.
❖ Adjust any of the settings provided in the third step of the preceding Set up a Focus.
Utilize both text and graphics.

USE THE IPAD'S ON-SCREEN KEYBOARD TO TYPE

The iPad's touchscreen keyboard allows you to input and modify text.

To type text, you may also utilize Dictation, an additional keyboard, and an Apple Pencil.

Tap any key to begin typing.

The Mail app opens with a blank email. The bottom portion of the screen contains the onscreen keyboard.

USE THE ON-SCREEN KEYBOARD TO TYPE TEXT

Tap a text field to bring up the onscreen keyboard in any app that lets you edit text. To type, you may either squeeze the keyboard closed to make it smaller, hit individual keys, or utilize QuickPath, which allows you to text by just sliding your finger from a single character to the other without lifting it (not accessible for all languages). Lift your finger to conclude a word. (Tapping the Delete key ⌫ erases the whole word if you slide to enter it.)

For convenient one-handed typing, you may drag the tiny keypad from the bottom of the screen to any desired location.

Pinch open to bring up the full-size keyboard again. You text by tapping keys on the full-size keyboard.

You may use the full-size keyboard and the tiny keyboard to perform any of the following while typing text:

* To type capital letters, slide to the letter after touching or tapping the Shift key ⇧.
* To activate Caps Lock, double-press the Shift button ⇧.
* Put a period + space at the end of a phrase quickly: Hit the Space bar twice.
* Put punctuation, symbols, or numbers here: Either touch the Symbols # + = or Numbers keys 123.
* To ensure proper spelling, either write the correction or touch the suggestion to replace a misspelled word (highlighted in red).
* Undo autocorrect: When you type, words that are misspelled are automatically fixed and briefly highlighted to let you know what's changed. To go back to the original spelling, just touch the underlined word and then hit the replacement spelling.
* Reverse the previous edit: Use three fingers to swipe left, and then hit the Undo button or the Undo icon ↰ at the very top of the screen.
* Remake the previous edit: Use three fingers to swipe right, then hit the Redo button or the Redo icon ↱ at the very top of the screen.

* Press the Hide Keypad key ⌨ to hide the on-screen keyboard.

ACTIVATE THE KEYBOARD'S SOUNDS

You may hear clicking while you write by customizing the keyboard settings.

Select Sounds from the Settings ⚙ menu, then activate Keyboard Clicks.

MAKE A TOUCHPAD OUT OF THE ON-SCREEN KEYBOARD

To make moving and positioning the insertion point easier, you may convert the onscreen keyboard onto a trackpad.

Slide your finger over the keyboard to move the insertion point.

Within the Notes app, a document is open. Trackpad mode is enabled on the onscreen keyboard located in the lower portion of the screen.

* Press and hold the spaces key with a single finger until a faint grey tint appears on the keyboard.

- ❖ Use your finger to move the point of insertion around the keyboard.
- ❖ Using a second finger to contact and hold the keypad while selecting text, move the first finger about the keyboard to fine-tune the selection.

WHEN TYPING, ADD LETTERS WITH ACCENTS OR OTHER CHARACTERS

To type a desired character, press and hold the corresponding letter, quantity, or symbol on the keyboard.

To input é, for instance, hold down the e-keyboard key, then glide your finger over and let go of the desired selection.

The alternative accented characters show up when you press and hold the E key on the onscreen keyboard.

Moreover, you may carry out one of the following:

❖ Using a Thai keyboard: Touch and hold the corresponding Arabic number to choose native numerals.

❖ Using a Chinese, Japanese, / Arabic keyboard: Slide left to see more choices; tap a recommended character or candidates at the very top of the keyboard to type it.

Note: Tap the right-up arrow to see the complete list of candidates. Press the down arrow to get back to the shortlist.

TRANSFER TEXT

❖ Choose the text you wish to move in an editing software.

❖ The chosen text may be moved inside the app by touching and holding it until it lifts.

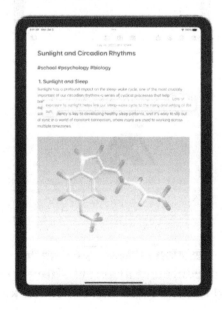

Within the Notes app, a document is open. Within the document, selected text may be lifted and transferred to a new spot.

Lift the finger before dragging, and drag the written content off the screen, if you decide not to move it.

CONFIGURE THE TYPING SETTINGS

Special typing functions, such as auto-correction and predictive text, may be turned on and off.

❖ Press and hold the Emoji key☺ or press the Switch Keyboard button🌐 while typing on the display keyboard, then choose Keyboard Settings. Or choose Keyboard under Settings⚙ > General.

❖ You may toggle the typing features on and off (green is on) (below All Keyboards).

DICTATING TEXT

You may dictate text anyplace you can write it using the iPad's Dictation app. With Dictation, you may utilize handwriting or typing. To input and modify text during Dictation, you may effortlessly transition between speaking & typing or scribbling by keeping the tools palette or keyboard open. For instance, you may use your voice to change text that you've selected using touch or pencil.

There is no need for an internet connection since dictation requests are handled in several languages on your smartphone. Your dictated text could be transferred to the search operator so they can handle the search when you speak in a search box.

Note: Features may differ and dictation might not be accessible in all languages, nations, or areas.

There can be cellular data fees while utilizing Dictation.

ACTIVATE THE DICTATION

❖ Navigate to Keyboard under Settings > General.
❖ Activate the Dictation feature. When prompted, choose "Enable Dictation."
  Go to the Apple Security website or choose About Dictation and Privacy from the Dictation menu

DICTATING TEXT ON A DOCUMENT

❖ To position the point of insertion where you wish to start dictating text, tap within the text box.

Start to speak when this symbol appears.

Tap to turn Dictation on and off.

The Notes app has the onscreen keyboard open. When the Dictation icon at the bottom of the keyboard is chosen, the text field's insertion point is underneath the Dictation button.

❖ On the on-screen keyboard, or in any text area where it displays, tap the Dictate key 🎤.

❖ Start dictating your content when the Quit Dictation button 🎤 shows up above the insertion location.

❖ You may use any of the methods that follow to add a punctuation mark or an emoji, or to carry out basic formatting tasks:

✓ Emoji names, such as "heart emoji" or "car emoji," should be spoken.

✓ Declare the punctuation mark's name, for example, "exclamation point."

Note: As you dictate, Dictation automatically adds question marks, commas, and periods in the languages it supports. Go to Settings > General > Keyboard and choose Auto-Punctuation to disable automatic punctuation. The set of formatting and punctuation instructions that you may use with Dictation is shown below.

Consider a formatting instruction like "new line" or "new paragraph."

❖ When you're finished, use the Quit Dictation button 🎤 . Alternatively, the Dictation will end on its own after 30 seconds of silence.

Dictation may be used in the language you use as well when using a keyboard for that language.

SWITCH OFF THE DICTATION

❖ Navigate to Keyboard under Settings 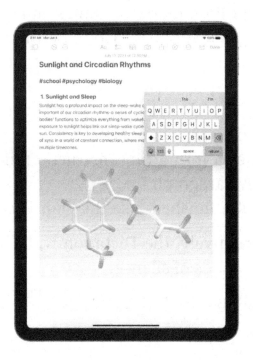 > General.
❖ Disable the dictation feature.

HOW TO REPOSITION THE ONSCREEN KEYBOARD

You can use the onscreen keyboard to text in three different ways on your iPad: split at the bottom, undocked in the center, or floating and moveable on the screen, depending on the model.

EMPLOY A FLOATING KEYBOARD

By sliding from the screen's bottom, you may make the keyboard that is displayed float and move wherever on the screen.

In the Notes app, there's an open note. Tiny and floating in the upper-right corner of the screen is the onscreen keyboard.

❖ To access the onscreen keyboard, tap within a text box.

❖ Slide the finger to Floating on the Hide Keypad key ⌨, touch and hold it, and then release it. You may drag and drop the little keyboard that appears to move around the screen.

❖ Use the (not accessible for all languages) to type by sliding your finger from a single character to the next while tapping the keys.

❖ You may pinch the floating versions open to bring the keyboard back to its full width.

ACTIVATE THE SPLIT KEYBOARD

To activate the Split Keyboard feature on models that enable it, perform one of the following:

❖ To enable or disable Split Keyboard, go to Settings > General > Keyboard.

❖ Press and hold the Emojis icon 😊 or the Globe Keypad key 🌐, and pick Split Keyboard from the Keyboard Settings menu.

DIVIDE THE KEYBOARD IN HALF

After enabling Split Keyboard in Settings, you may do any of these actions by tapping in a text field to bring up the onscreen keyboard:

❖ To divide the keyboard, press and hold the Conceal Keypad key ⌨, move your finger to the Split button, and then let go of it.

❖ Reassemble the divided keyboard as follows: Touch and hold ⌨. Slide the finger toward Merge, then let go of the Hide Keypad key that you touched and held.

UNDOCKING THE KEYBOARD

You may undock the keyboard (that is accessible on models with support for Split Keyboard) so that it rises from the bottom of the display when Split Keypad is enabled in Settings.

❖ To access the onscreen keyboard, tap within a text box.

❖ Hold down the Hide Keypad key ⌨ with your finger, move it to Undock, and then let go.
The keyboard rises from the screen's bottom. In this posture, you may use the keyboard to type.

❖ Hold down the Hide Keypad key, move your finger to Dock, and then release it to bring the undocked keyboard back to its original place.

SELECTING, CUTTING, COPYING, & PASTING TEXT

The iPad's touchscreen keyboard may be used to choose and modify text in fields of text inside applications.

CHOOSE AND MODIFY TEXT

❖ Take any of these actions to choose text:

  ✓ Choose a word: Tap twice with a single finger.

  ✓ Choose a paragraph: With one finger, tap three times.

  ✓ Choose a passage of text: Drag towards the last phrase in the block after double-tapping and holding the initial word.

Move the grab points to adjust the selection.

Tap to cut, copy, or paste selected text.

In the Notes app, text is chosen inside a note. There is a menu with buttons like Cut, Copy, & Paste above the text that has been chosen. Grab points are provided at each end of the highlighted text to allow you to modify the selection.

❖ When you've chosen the text that you want to alter, you have the choice to type or touch the selection to view the edit options:

159

- ✓ Cut: Tap Cut once, or squeeze closed twice with three fingers.
- ✓ Copy: Pinch shut with three fingers, or tap copy.
- ✓ Paste: Pinch reveal with three fingers, or tap Paste.
- ✓ Replace: See the recommended text to replace it with, or ask Siri to provide one.
- ✓ B/I/U: Arrange the chosen text.
- ✓ ▶ See further choices.

Advice: Touch and hold the chosen text until it pops up, then drag it to a new spot to relocate it without cutting or copying.

TYPING TEXT

❖ Choose one of the following methods to place the text insertion point:
- ✓ Wherever you'd like to add text, tap.
- ✓ Press and hold to enlarge the text, then drag to adjust the insertion place.

A notation indicating the location of the insertion point for any text that is modified or added. Placing the insertion point is made simpler by enlarging the surrounding text.

❖ **Note:** To find the text that you want to edit in a lengthy document, press and hold its right edge and drag your scroller to get there.

❖ To add text, just type or paste it.

SAVING KEYSTROKES USING TEXT SUBSTITUTIONS

Create a text replacement on your iPad so you may type a word or phrase in with a short string of letters. For instance, to enter "On my way!" type "omw." You have already got that one set up, but you may add others as well.

MAKE A SUBSTITUTE TEXT

❖ Take one of these actions:
  ✓ Using an on-screen keyboard: Press and hold the Switch Keyboard⊕ or Emoji button☺, choose Keyboard Settings, and finally SELECT Text Replacement.
  ✓ Using a separate keyboard: Toggle between Text Replacement and General Keyboard under Settings⊚ > General.
❖ In the upper right corner, tap the Add button ✛.
❖ In the Phrase area, type your desired text shortcut, and in the Shortcut field, type your phrase.

DO YOU WANT A TERM OR PHRASE THAT YOU USE TO BE CORRECTED?

❖ Toggle between Text Replacement and General Keyboard under Settings ⊚ > General.
❖ In the Phrase area, type your word or phrase; leave the Shortcuts field empty. Then, tap the Add button ✛ in the upper right corner.

MAKE A TEXT SUBSTITUTE FOR THE SUPPLIED PAIRS AND WORDS

For word and input pairings, you may generate a text replacement when using expected Chinese or Japanese keyboards. You now have the text replacement in your dictionary. The associated word and input are used in place of the shortcut when you use a compatible keyboard to enter the text shortcuts for the word or input.

There are shortcuts accessible for the following:

* Pinyin for Simplified Chinese
* Mandarin (Traditional): Pinyin and Zhuyin
* Japanese: Kana and Romaji

TO KEEP YOUR PRIVATE VOCABULARY CURRENT ACROSS ALL OF YOUR DEVICES, USE ICLOUD

After selecting Settings ⚙> [your username] > the iCloud, activate iCloud Drive.

RESET YOUR DICTIONARY

* Select Reset Keyboard Dictionary after going to Settings ⚙> General > Transfer / Reset iPad > Reset.
* In the keyboard dictionary, tap Reset.
  The keyboard dictionary reverts to its original configuration and any customized terms and shortcuts are eliminated.

ADAPT OR ADD KEYBOARDS TO THE IPAD

On your iPad, you may install keyboards to write on or use Dictation in many languages. The arrangement of your external or onscreen keyboard may also be altered.

You can type in multiple languages without switching keyboards if you install keyboards for additional languages. The two dialects you utilize most often are automatically switched between on your keyboard. (Not accessible in every language.)

TO ADD OR DELETE A MULTILINGUAL KEYBOARD

❖ Navigate to Keyboard under Settings ⚙ > General.
❖ Click Keyboards, then do one of the following actions:
  ✓ *Adding a keyboard*: After selecting the keyboard from the list, tap Add New Keyboard. Continue to add keyboards.
  ✓ *Removing a keyboard*: To delete a keyboard, choose Edit, then press the delete icon ⊖ next to the desired keyboard. Finally, select Done.
  ✓ *Reorganize the list of keys on your keyboard*: Select Edit, move the Reorder icon ☰ next to the keyboard to a different location in the list, and then select Done.

A keyboard for an additional language is added, and it instantly gets added to the list of preferred languages. Go to Settings> General > Languages and Region to see and directly add languages to this list. Additionally, you may rearrange the list to modify the text appearance on applications and websites.

USE A DIFFERENT KEYBOARD

On the keyboard that appears on the screen: Press and hold the Emojis icon or the Switch Keypad key, and then choose the desired keyboard by tapping its name.

Additionally, you may switch between keyboards by using the Emoji button and the Switch Keyboard key. Tap again to view different keyboards that are enabled.

To switch between English, emojis, and any keyboards you add for more languages on an external keyboard, hold down Control, or then tap the Space bar.

You may also use the move Keyboard key on the Magic keypad for iPad & Smart Keyboard to quickly move between keyboards.

PROVIDE YOUR KEYBOARD WITH A DIFFERENT LAYOUT

If your keyboard's key layout isn't compatible with another one, you may use one instead.

❖ Navigate to Keyboards > General > Keypad > Settings.
❖ After tapping a language at the very top of the display, choose a different layout from the selection.

SNAPPING A SCREENSHOT

To examine what shows up on the screen of your iPad later, distribute it with other people, or connect it to documents, take a photo of it.

USING AN IPAD WITH FACE ID, TAKE A SCREENSHOT

Simultaneously push and release both the volume button and the top button.

❖ Your screen briefly displays a thumbnail of the picture in the lower-left corner.

To see the screenshot, tap its thumbnail; to dismiss it, slide left.

❖ Two iPad devices with Face ID are shown in an illustration. Arrows indicate the volume and top buttons.

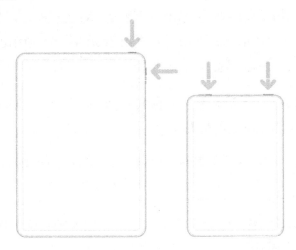

Screenshots in the Photos application are immediately saved to the image library. To see every one of your pictures in one location, open Photos and choose Screenshots from the sidebar menu, located under Media Types.

WITH A DEVICE THAT HAS TOUCH ID, TAKE A SCREENSHOT

❖ Press and hold both the Home and the top buttons simultaneously.

Your screen briefly displays a thumbnail of the snapshot in the lower-left corner.

❖ To see the screenshot, tap its thumbnail; to dismiss it, slide left.

A screenshot of an iPad that has Touch ID. The Home and top buttons are indicated by arrows

Screenshots in the Pictures app are immediately saved to the picture library. To see every one of your snapshots in one location, open Photos and choose Screenshots from the sidebar menu, located under Media Types.

GET A SCREENSHOT OF THE WHOLE PAGE

Content that fills your iPad screen, like a whole website in Safari, may be snapped as a screenshot.

❖ Choose from the following options:
  ✓ If your iPad has Face ID, quickly push and release both the volume up and down buttons at the same time.

✓ Press and let go of the top key and the button for Home simultaneously on an iPad that has a home button.

❖ On the screen, tap the thumbnail of the screenshot located in the lower-left corner.

❖ Select the following after selecting Full Page and Done:

✓ To save a screenshot to your Photos collection , tap Save to Photos.

✓ To save a screenshot in the File application , choose a location, hit Save PDF to Files, and then touch Save.

USE THE IPAD TO RECORD YOUR SCREEN

It is possible to record what occurs on the screen of your iPad.

❖ Navigate to Settings > Control Centre and choose Screen Recording by tapping the Insert button .

❖ After launching Control Centre and selecting the Screen Recording option , watch for the 3-second timeout.

❖ Open Control Centre, press the red status indicator at the very top of the screen or the Selected Screens Recording button, then hit the Stop button to end the recording.

The Photos app automatically stores screen recordings in your photo collection. Open Photos and choose Screen Recordings from the Photos sidebar, located under Media Types, to see all of the screen captures in one location.

CHAPTER FOUR

CONFIGURE IPAD FAMILY SHARING

You may share the use of Apple services, buys, an iCloud data storage plan, and other features with up to five additional family members with Family Sharing. Even your lost gadgets may be found together.

Other family members are invited to join by the organizer, an adult member of the family. Family Sharing is automatically configured on all devices when family members join. Subsequently, the collective decides which features and services to use and distribute.

The screen under Settings for Family Sharing. Above the common characteristics is a list of five family members.

MAKE A GROUP CALLED FAMILY SHARING

Family Sharing only requires one device to be set up. After that, it is accessible on any device you have logged in with an identical Apple ID.

❖ To create your Family Sharing group, go to Settings ⚙ > [your name] > Family and follow the prompts on the screen.

❖ Include a family member or relatives. An adult member of the family may be added and designated as a parent/guardian.

  Later on, family members may be added as well.

❖ To set up a feature for your group for Family Sharing, tap it and then follow the directions on the screen.

  For a youngster to enable Apple Cash or parental controls, touch the feature, press the child's name, and then follow the on-screen instructions

  Sharing options may be changed at any moment, and you can see what you're sharing with your family.

TAKE A PERSON OUT OF OR ADD THEM BACK TO AN IPAD FAMILY-SHARING GROUP

Family members (apart from teenagers with parental restrictions or children) have the option to withdraw themselves from a Family Shared group, as well as the group organizer's ability to do so.

ELIMINATE A FAMILY MEMBER FROM THE GROUP

Any member of a shared family group may be removed by the group organizer. A family member's access to pooled subscriptions and material acquired by other members is instantly terminated upon their removal.

❖ Navigate to Family under Settings.
❖ After selecting [member's name], choose Remove [member's name] from Family.

It is not possible to take a youngster out of your family-sharing group. You may, however, transfer them to a different group or remove their Apple ID.

To remove an adolescent from the group, you must first turn off the display time setting if they were enabled.

EXIT A FAMILY SHARING COMMUNITY

You quit sharing all your purchases and memberships with family members when you depart from a Family Shared group, and you no longer have access to any shared material.

Reminder: The Family Share group organizer cannot go. You must dissolve the group and have an additional adult form a new one if you desire to change organizers.

❖ Navigate to Family under Settings.
❖ Select Stop Utilizing Family Sharing after tapping [your name].

DISBAND THE FAMILY SHARING COMMUNITY

All members of the family are eliminated from the group simultaneously when the family planner disables Family Sharing. All members instantly lose access to the shared material and subscriptions when a Family Shared group is dissolved.

❖ Navigate to [your name] under Settings ⚙ > Family.
❖ Click to Abandon Family Sharing.

UTILIZE APPLE CARD AND CASH WITH IPAD FAMILY SHARING (U.S. ONLY)

With your group on Family Sharing, you may utilize Apple Card and Apple Cash. A child's Apple Cash account may be established by a Family Sharing group organizer, who can also distribute Apple Cards to dependable group members.

ENROLL A KID IN THE APPLE CASH FAMILY

A youngster may have Apple Cash set up for them by the family organizer.

❖ Navigate to Family under Settings.
❖ Select the kid you want to add Apple Cash to by tapping on them.
❖ Press Apple Cash and adhere to the instructions shown on the screen.

To view the card balance, keep an eye on transactions, and restrict the recipients the kid may transfer money to, navigate to Settings> Wallet. Check out Apple Cash Management.

CREATE AN APPLE CARD FAMILY ACCOUNT

For youngsters who are 13 years of age or older, you may manage payments, share the Apple Card with relatives, and adjust account settings and limitations. Each person's information may be managed and reviewed as well.

❖ Open Settings > Families > Share My Apple Card. Only with an Apple Card does the choice show up.
❖ Pay attention to the directions shown on the screen.

SCREEN TIME

START USING IPAD SCREEN TIME NOW

Screen Time provides you and your loved ones with information on how you and your members use your devices, including the apps and websites that you visit and how frequently you pick them up.

Select App and Website Activity from the Settings ⚙ > Screen Time menu, then select Turn On to activate the feature.

ACTIVATE THE SCREEN TIME

Select App and Website Activity from the Settings ⚙ > Screen Time menu, then select Turn on App and Website Activity.

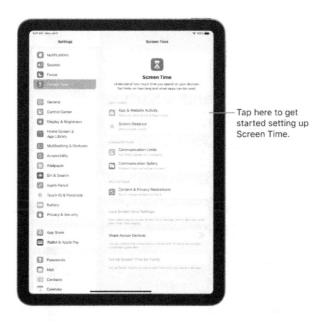

Tap here to get started setting up Screen Time.

The page that appears when you first set up page Time indicates that you should tap App and Website Activity.

APPLY SCREEN TIME TO ALL OF YOUR GADGETS

All of your devices that are logged in with the same Apple ID allow you to share your display time settings and reports.

❖ Go to Screen Time under Settings.

❖ After swiping down, activate Share Across Devices.

SEE THE SUMMARY OF YOUR SCREEN TIME

You may read a report of the apps you use at any time once you enable App & Website Activity. It includes information on how much time you spend using different app categories, how often you take up your iPad along with other devices, which applications are the most notification-heavy, and more.

❖ Go to Screen Time under Settings.
❖ After selecting View All App and Website Activity, choose one of the following actions:
   ✓ To get an overview of your weekly use, tap Week.
   ✓ To get an overview of your daily use, tap Day.

a weekly analysis from Screen Time that breaks out the overall time spent using apps by both app category and app.

TO QUICKLY ASSESS HOW MUCH TIME YOU SPEND ON YOUR SMARTPHONE, UTILIZE THE SCREEN TIME WIDGET

By including Screen Time widgets on your Home Screen, you can easily monitor how much time you spend on your devices. Your Screen Time summary is shown in the widget; the more widgets you install, the greater the data it shows.

You can use Family Sharing to set up time on the computer for family members. By tapping the widget, you can get a list of everyone in your family group. To access a family member's report, tap their name.

CONFIGURE IPAD SCREEN TIME

You can plan screen-free time, impose time limitations on app usage, and more using Screen Time.

SET ASIDE TIME TO SPEND AWAY FROM SCREENS

When you want to take a break from your gadgets, you may stop alerts and applications. You may want to plan downtime for when you eat or go to bed, for instance.

Only the calls, texts, and applications you approve are accessible during downtime. During downtime, you may use applications you've opted to allow at all times and receive calls from people you've chosen to allow communication with.

❖ Go to Screen Time under Settings ⚙.
❖ If you haven't already, switch on App and Website Activity by tapping on it.
❖ After selecting Downtime, do the following actions:
  ✓ Click on Activate Downtime Until Tomorrow.
  ✓ To plan for downtime, tap Scheduled.

A five-minute notice is sent out before the start of the downtime when it is scheduled. You have two options: either turn off downtime until the start of the planned downtime or disregard the reminder.

❖ After choosing Customize Days or Every Day, choose the start and finish hours.

By disabling Scheduled, you may always stop the Downtime schedule.

LIMIT THE USAGE OF APPS

Both individual applications and categories of apps (such as games and social networking) may have time limits imposed.

❖ Go to Screen Time under Settings ⊚ .
❖ Select Add Limit from the App Limits menu.
❖ Choose one or more categories for apps.
  You may set limitations for certain applications by selecting the apps you wish to limit after tapping the name of the category to see all of the applications in that category. The time restriction you choose applies to all of the categories or applications you pick.
❖ After selecting Next, enter the allotted time.
  To establish a time restriction for every day, choose Customize Days and then establish daily limitations.
❖ After defining all the parameters, click Add.

SELECT CONTACTS AND APPLICATIONS TO ALWAYS ALLOW

Even during downtime, you may choose which applications to use and which contacts to keep in touch with at all times—for instance, in case of an emergency.

❖ Navigate to Always Permitted under Settings ⚙ > Screen Time.

❖ To add or delete an app from the list of allowed apps, press ⊕ or ⊖ next to it underneath Allowed Apps.

❖ Tap Contacts to choose the contacts you'd like to provide communication access to.
This is the option that you choose under Communication Limits. You may choose any of the following after changing this option to Specific Contacts:

✓ Select One From My Contacts: to choose which individuals to permit communication with.

✓ Add New Person: To add contact and make that individual available for conversation.

❖ On the upper left, press the Back button ‹.

CHAPTER FIVE

APPLE PAY AND WALLET

CONFIGURE IPAD FOR APPLE PAY

To make safe payments in applications and on sites that accept Apple Pay, set up Apple Pay. (Available in some countries and areas; refer to the list of nations and locations that accept Apple Pay.)

INCLUDE A DEBIT OR CREDIT CARD

❖ Go to Set up and utilize Apple Card on iPads (U.S. only) to add Apple Card. Follow these steps for additional debit and credit cards:
After selecting Wallet and Apple Pay in Settings, choose Add Card. You may be prompted to use your Apple ID to log in.

❖ Take any of the following actions:
✓ Include a fresh card: Select Debit and Credit Card, hit Next, then either manually input the card information or move your card around so it shows up in the frame.
✓ Include your earlier cards: Select any card you've already used by tapping Previous Cards. These cards might be the ones linked to your Apple ID, the cards you use on other devices for Apple Pay, the cards you included in Safari AutoFill or the cards you took out of Wallet. Press Proceed, verify using Touch ID or Face ID and then adhere to the prompts shown on the screen.

✓ Use a compatible app to add a card: Select the app from your bank or credit card company (see From Applications on Your iPad below).

When determining if your card qualifies for Apple Pay, the card issuer may need more information from you to finish the verification process.

CONFIGURE THE DEFAULT CARD

Your primary payment card is the first one you add. Anytime you like, you may change the default card to anything else.

Navigate to Settings⚙ > Wallet and Apple Pay, and choose a card by tapping Default Card.

CONFIGURE AND USE IPAD APPLE CASH (U.S. ONLY)

You may send, request, and get back money using the Messages app, use Apple Pay to make purchases and transfer your iPhone Cash balance to a bank account.

LAUNCH APPLE PAY

Take one of the following actions:

❖ To activate Apple Cash, go to Settings > Wallet and Apple Pay.
❖ Send or receive a payment over Messages.

USE APPLE CASH TO MAKE PURCHASES

Anywhere that takes a Visa and has Apple Pay capability can accept Apple Cash.

TAKE PAYMENTS WITH APPLE CASH

The amount of money you get is added to the Apple Cash account. You have the option of accepting payments manually or automatically.

- ❖ Select Apple Cash after selecting Settings > Wallet and Apple Pay.
- ❖ Select a single option from the following:
  - ✓ Accept Payments Automatically
  - ✓ Take Payments by Hand
    Payments are refunded to the sender within seven days if they are not accepted.

CHECK YOUR TRANSACTIONS AND BALANCE

To check your balance, go to Settings ⚙ > Wallet and Apple Pay and hit Apple Cash.

Other options include the following:

- ❖ Check out your transactions: Select Transactions. To see the transactions you made sorted by year, scroll down.
- ❖ Obtain a declaration: After swiping down, choose "Request Transaction Statement."

HOW TO HANDLE YOUR APPLE CASH

Select Apple Cash after selecting Wallet and Apple Pay under Settings. You may then perform the following:

❖ Transfer funds with a debit card. You may configure Auto Reload as well.
❖ Make a bank transfer. To learn how to transfer money from Apple Cash to a bank account / Visa debit card, see the Apple Help page.
❖ Revise the details of your bank account.
❖ Speak with Apple Support.
❖ Create an Apple Cash account and use it for family-sharing group members under the age of 18. See How to Set Up a Child's Apple Cash Family.
❖ To service your account and raise your transaction limitations, you must authenticate your identity.

APPLE CARD SETUP AND USE ON AN IPAD (U.S. ONLY)

The Apple Cards is a form of credit that the company developed to assist you in living a better financial life. Within minutes, you may register for an Apple Card on your iPad and begin making purchases in-store, via applications, and online anywhere in the globe with Apple Pay. With Apple Card, you can easily monitor your balance and recent transactions in real-time. You can also get help for your card at any time by sending a text message from Messages.

ACQUIRE AN APPLE CARD

- Select Add Card from the Wallet and Apple Pay menu, then select Apply to Apple Card.
- To submit your application, fill out the form and accept the terms and conditions.
- Examine the terms of your Apple card offer, such as the APR and credit limit, and decide whether to accept or reject it.
- You may do any one of the following if you agree to the terms:
  - ✓ Make Apple Card your primary payment method for purchases made with Apple Pay.
  - ✓ To use in locations where Apple Pay isn't accepted, get an actual Apple Card.

MAKE USE OF YOUR APPLE CARD

You may use your iPad's Apple Card to make Apple Pay transactions online or via applications.

Additionally, Apple Card may be used in places that do not accept Apple Pay:

- Through phone calls, online browsers, or apps: To check the card number, expiry date, and security code, go to Settings ⚙ > Wallet & Apple Pay, choose Apple Card, and then select Card Information. Utilize this information when placing your order.
- Utilize the titanium card at restaurants, shops, and other establishments.

EXAMINE THE TRANSACTIONS AND STATEMENTS

Select Apple Card from Wallet and Apple Pay in Settings, then do one of the following actions:

❖ Examine your purchases: To see all of your transactions arranged by year, swipe down or tap Transactions, after which you may examine your most recent transactions.

❖ Obtain statements every month: To see the amount, recent purchases, payments, and credits, tap the Card amount. To see the monthly statements, scroll down. You may export activities to a CSV, OFX, QFX, and QBO file, download the PDF, or click a statement to view a summary for that month.

MAKE THE NECESSARY PAYMENTS

Select Apple Card from Wallet and Apple Pay in Settings, then do one of the following actions:

❖ Pay dates: After selecting Pay My Bill and Pay Different Amount and entering the payment information (for instance, the account & date), choose Scheduled Payments and authenticate with your password, Face ID, or Touch ID.

❖ Pay once: Select Make a Payment, move the checkmark to change the amount, or select Show Keypad to input the amount, choose Pay Now and Pay Later, check the payment information (including the payment account), and then verify using Touch ID, Face ID, or your password.

UTILIZE THE HOME SCREEN WIDGET FOR APPLE CARDS

You can quickly see the Apple Card balance, available credit, and spending activities with the help of the Apple Card widget.

❖ Make your Home Screen a home for the Apple Card widget.
❖ Pick Weekly, Monthly, and Yearly from the menu after touching and holding the widget to see the spending behavior for a particular period.
❖ Tap the widget to see and manage your Apple Card.

CHECK APPLE CARD DATA, ADJUST PREFERENCES, GET IN TOUCH WITH HELP, AND MORE

Select Apple Card from Wallet and Apple Pay in Settings, and then do one of the following actions:

❖ Set transaction restrictions, share the Apple Card among family members, and do a lot more.
❖ Control your monthly Apple Card installments.
❖ Examine the upcoming payments.
❖ Check out the credit information.
❖ Delete or add connected bank accounts.
❖ Request a replacement titanium card by locking or unlocking it.
❖ Modify the notification preferences.
❖ Make changes to your billing address.
❖ Get assistance over the phone, via messages,

CONTROL APPLE PAY CARDS & ACTIVITY

You can control the cards you utilize for Apple Pay & see a history of your recent purchases under Settings.

SEE A CARD'S DETAILS AND ADJUST ITS SETTINGS

❖ Navigate to Wallet and Apple Pay under Settings.
❖ After tapping a card, you may choose to:
  ✓ To see your recent history, tap Transactions. Turn off Display History to conceal this information. View your whole Apple Pay history by consulting your card issuer's statement.
  ✓ See the last four numbers of your device account number (the number sent to the merchant) and your card number.
  ✓ Modify the billing address.
  ✓ Don't use the card with Apple Pay.

MODIFY THE APPLE PAY CONFIGURATION

❖ Navigate to Wallet and Apple Pay under Settings.
❖ Take one of the following actions:
  ✓ Decide on your default card.
  ✓ For purchases, provide the contact details and the shipment address.

IF THE IPAD HAS BEEN MISPLACED OR STOLEN, TAKE YOUR CARDS OUT OF APPLE PAY

You may use Find My to assist find and safeguard your iPad if you enable it.

Choose one of the following actions to take your cards out of Apple Pay:

❖ Log in to the Apple ID account on a Mac or PC. Choose the iPad that was lost from the Devices section. Click Remove Items in the Wallet and Apple Pay section.
❖ On a different iPad or iPhone: click the missing iPad by going to Settings > [your name], then click Remove Contents (below Wallet and Apple Pay).
❖ Give your card issuers a call.

You may put cards back later if you delete them.

All of your debit and credit cards used for Apple Pay on your iPad are deleted if you sign away from iCloud under Settings > [your name]. When the following time you log in, you may add the cards once again.

CHAPTER SIX

ACCESSORIES

IPAD CHARGING CORD AND POWER ADAPTER

With the accompanying USB-C power converter and charging cable, you may connect your iPad to a power source and use it to charge its battery. The model of your iPad and the place you live determine the size and kind of adapter. Your iPad model determines the kind of charging cord you need.

In addition, the charging cable may be used to connect your iPad to your Mac to charge it, transfer data, and utilize it as an additional display.

USB-C CHARGING CABLE

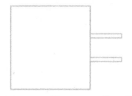

The power adaptor for USB-C

USB-C CHARGING CABLE

The Charge Cable for USB-C

USB-C TO LIGHTNING CABLE

The USB-C to Lightning Cable

UTILIZE IPAD AND AIRPODS TOGETHER

You can utilize AirPods (separately sold) to listen to music playing on your iPad, make and take FaceTime calls, read and reply to messages, get reminders when needed, and much more. You may additionally utilize AirPods to hear discussions more easily in loud surroundings

CONNECT AIRPODS TO YOUR IPAD

* ❖ Turn on Bluetooth on your iPad by going to Settings ⚙ > Bluetooth.
* ❖ Navigate to the iPad Home Screen.
* ❖ Take any of the following actions:
    * ✓ First, second, and third generation AirPods as well as AirPods Pro: With the AirPods inside, open the case and place it next to your tablet.
    * ✓ AirPods Max: Remove the Smart Case from your AirPods Max and place them next to the device.

- ❖ After following the on-screen directions, choose Done.

  Note: Go to Settings> Bluetooth, then choose your AirPods Max if the on-screen instructions to link them don't show up. Hold down the noise management button on the AirPods Max until the status indicator turns white.

All of your compatible devices that are logged in with the same Apple ID that you use (iOS 10, iPadOS 13, macOS 10.12, watchOS 3, or later necessary) will automatically connect your AirPods with them.

COMPATIBILITY OF IPAD MODELS WITH APPLE PENCIL

Learn which Apple Pencil is compatible with your iPad.

THE SECOND-GENERATION APPLE PENCIL

Second-generation Apple Pencil

The following models are compatible with the Apple Pencil (2nd generation):

- ❖ iPad mini (6th gen)
- ❖ Fourth-generation iPad Air and subsequent models
- ❖ 11-inch iPad Pro (all versions)
- ❖ 12.9-inch iPad Pro (3rd generation & later)

HOW TO TYPE TEXT WITH SCRIBBLE

You may type text on compatible models using Scribble and an Apple Pencil (separately available). You can send yourself a reminder, respond to messages fast, and do more without having to launch the app or use the onscreen keyboard. Your writing remains confidential as Scribble instantly translates what you write to text on your iPad.

Note: There are several languages available for Scribble. Visit the page for iOS & iPadOS Feature Availability.

TO INPUT TEXT IN ANY TYPE OF FIELD, USE AN APPLE PENCIL

❖ When you write with an apple pen in a text field, Scribble will automatically type your handwriting. Even if your handwriting stretches over the text field's boundaries, Scribble still functions.

❖ You may touch the Scribble toolbar to perform an action shortcut. Depending on the software you're using, other actions may be available, such as the Undo ↺ and Show Keyboard ⌨ buttons. To have the toolbar authored while you type text, hit the Ellipsis button ⋯ and go on to select Auto-minimize. Tap the smaller version of the toolbar to bring it up in full.

TO INPUT TEXT IN NOTE AND FREEFORM, USE AN APPLE PENCIL

❖ To see the tool palette, turn off the Markup Switch Ⓐ icon in Notes or Freeform.

❖ Select the Handwriting tool (located to the left of the pencil) from the tool panel.

❖ When you write with an Apple Pencil, Scribble will automatically type your handwriting.

USE THE APPLE PENCIL TO SELECT AND EDIT TEXT

Using Apple Pencil & Scribble, you may input text in the following ways:

❖ Eliminate a word: Mark it out.

❖ Put text here: Write in the blank spot that appears when you hold your finger in a text area.

❖ Combine or divide characters: Make a line that is vertical between both.

❖ To pick a text and see editing options, either draw a circle around it or underline it. Drag from the start or finish of the chosen text to modify the selection.

❖ Choose a word: Tap the word twice.

❖ Choose a paragraph: You may either move the Apple Pencil across the text or triple-tap any word inside it.

USE THE HOMEPOD ALONGSIDE ADDITIONAL WIRELESS SPEAKERS TO STREAM AUDIO FROM AN IPAD

Wireless devices such as HomePod, Apple TV, smart TVs with AirPlay 2, and Bluetooth® speakers and headphones can all play audio from iPads.

UTILIZE AN IPAD TO PLAY AUDIO ON A WIRELESS DEVICE

❖ Open an audio player on your iPad, such as Music or Podcasts , and choose a file to play.

❖ Select a playback destination by tapping the Playback Destination button .

Note: Verify that your AirPlay 2-capable devices are connected to the same Wi-Fi network if they don't show up in your list of playback destinations. If you transfer a Bluetooth-enabled item outside of its Bluetooth range, the iPad is the playback destination once again.

You may also hit the Playback Location button in the Control Centre or on the Lock Screen to choose the playback destination.

PLAY MUSIC ACROSS MANY AIRPLAY 2-CAPABLE DEVICES

You may play music on many AirPlay 2-capable devices linked to the same WiFi connection using iPad and AirPlay 2. For instance, you may stream a party playlist to HomePod speaker in the kitchen and living room, an

Apple TV in your bedroom, and a smart TV within the den using AirPlay 2.

Siri: Say anything along these lines:

❖ "Cease to play music everywhere."
❖ "Decide to turn down the dining room noise to 10%."
❖ "What song is on in the kitchen?"
❖ "Audience a song I enjoy in the kitchen."
❖ Include the speaker in the living room.
❖ "Take the music out of the kitchen."
❖ "To the den, move the music."

Additionally, you may choose playback locations directly from the iPad display.

❖ In the Control Centre, on your Lock Screen, or on the Presently Playing screen for the application you are now using, tap the Playback Destinations button.
❖ Choose the devices you want to utilize.
   Note: A stereo pair of devices is handled as a single sound device.

KEYBOARDS FOR IPADS

IPad keyboards (separately offered) protect the tablet and let you type using the full screen of the device.

Every keyboard fits the iPad exactly and closes to form a thin cover.

THE MAGIC KEYBOARD FOLIO AND MAGIC KEYBOARD

You can navigate across the iPad screen, launch applications, and do a lot more using the built-in trackpad of the Magic Keypad for iPad (which is compatible with iPad Air & iPad Pro) & Magic Keypad Folio (which is compatible with iPad 10th generation).

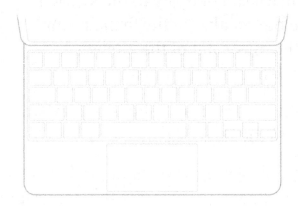

An example of the iPad Magic Keyboard

Navigate to Settings> General > Keypad > Hardware The keyboard, then move the slider to change the keyboard intensity of the magic keypad for iPad Air and iPad Pro.

Important: The iPad is held firmly in place by magnets included in the Magic Keyboard the Magic Keyboard Folio. Credit cards and hotel key cards are examples of cards that contain data on a magnetic strip. Do not place these cards on the iPad-attaching Magic Keyboard & Magic Keypad Folio surfaces as this might demagnetize them.

THE SMART KEYBOARD FOLIO AND SMART KEYBOARD

An example of a smart keyboard

There is no need for batteries or additional power for the Smart Keyboard & Smart Keyboard Folio.

USE THE IPAD AND AN EXTERNAL APPLE KEYBOARD TO DICTATE TEXT

Instead of inputting text on an iPhone external keyboard, you may dictate it.

Note: Features may differ and dictating may not be accessible in all languages, nations, or areas. There can be cellular data fees (Wi-Fi Plus Cellular models).

❖ Enable Dictation may be enabled by going to Settings 🔘 > General > Keyboard.

❖ Speak after tapping the Dictation button 🎤 located in the Shortcuts bar at the bottom of the screen.

❖ Press the Keyboard button ⌨ located at the bottom of the screen once you're done.

The iPad adds punctuation automatically as you talk to input text. Saying their names allows you to add emojis (such as "mind blown emoji" or "happy emoji").

Advice: Press the Switch Keypad key-D on the magical keyboard for iPad/Smart Keyboard to swiftly transition to dictation.

UTILIZE IPAD TO PRINT

AirPrint: Print wirelessly from applications like Mail, pictures, Safari, and Freeform to a printer that supports AirPrint. The App Store offers a large selection of applications that enable AirPrint.

The printer and iPad need to be connected to the same WiFi network.

PRINTING A DOCUMENT

According to the app you're using, touch the Share ⬆, More •••, Reply ↩, or Actions Menu ⌄ buttons before selecting Print. (If you don't see Print, swipe up.)

VIEW THE PRINT JOB'S STATUS

Tap Print Centre after launching the App Switcher.

The number of papers in the queue is shown by the label on the icon.

Choose the print job to cancel in Print Centre, then choose Cancel Printing.

CHAPTER SEVEN

PLAY WITH ADDITIONAL DEVICES

USE YOUR IPAD TO SHARE THE CONNECTION TO THE INTERNET (WI-FI + CELLULAR)

Your iPad's cellular internet connection may be shared with other devices using Personal Hotspot. When other devices lack a Wi-Fi network connection to the internet, a personal hotspot might be helpful.

Note: Not all carriers support Personal Hotspot. There can be additional costs. The iPad model and your carrier will determine how many devices may connect to your Personal Hotspot simultaneously. To learn more, get in touch with your carrier.

CONFIGURE IPAD PERSONAL HOTSPOT

Navigate to Settings ⚙ > Cellular, choose Set Up Private Hotspot, and then adhere to the instructions on the screen.

Note: If you have enabled Cellular Data under Setting > Cellular, but the Set Up Private Hotspot option is not visible, speak with your carrier about including Personal Hotspot in your plan.

UTILIZE YOUR PERSONAL HOTSPOT TO CONNECT A MAC OR PC

You may link a Mac or PC to the Personal Hotspot by Bluetooth®, USB, or Wi-Fi. Take one of the following actions:

❖ For connection from a Mac, use Wi-Fi: Refer to Connect iPads to the Internet.
❖ Connect via Wi-Fi using a PC: On your personal computer, subscribe to a Private Hotspot by following the manufacturer's instructions.
❖ Use USB: Refer to Use a cable to connect your iPad to your computer.
❖ To establish a connection from a Mac, go to the guide on using Bluetooth to link your Mac and even iPhone.
❖ Follow the manufacturer's instructions to establish a Bluetooth internet connection to connect from a PC.

LINK AN IPAD OR IPHONE TO YOUR PERSONAL HOTSPOT

Navigate to Settings > Wi-Fi on the second device, choose it from the available networks list, and then (if requested) input the Personal Hotspot password.

ALTER THE PASSWORD OR TURN OFF THE PERSONAL HOTSPOT

Navigate to Setting > Personal Hotspot and do one of the below actions:

- ❖ To modify the password, choose Wi-Fi Password and adhere to the prompts shown on the screen.
- ❖ Turn off Allow Another to Join and Turn Off Personal Hotspot. Every gadget using your private hotspot gets unplugged.

A blue band appears at the very top of your iPad screen and the Personal Hotspot symbol ⌒ shows in the connected Mac's status bar when a Mac is linked to your Personal Hotspot.

USING THE IPAD TO MAKE AND ACCEPT PHONE CALLS

With Wi-Fi Calling, you may use your iPhone to make and get calls on the iPad (iOS 9 or higher is needed).

There may be cellular costs. Some providers do not offer Wi-Fi calling.

Important: Wi-Fi Plus Cellular versions only offer cellular data transfer; they lack support for cellular phone service. You must utilize Wi-Fi Calling & an iPhone to make telephone calls using any model of iPad.

BEFORE STARTING

Perform the following actions on your iPad and other devices (iOS 9, iPad operating system 13, OS X 10.10, or higher, required):

- ❖ Configure FaceTime on your iPad and iPhone.
- ❖ Use the same Apple ID to log in to both devices.

PERMIT CALLS FROM YOUR IPHONE TO YOUR IPAD

You set up the iPad after setting up your iPhone.

❖ Navigate to Settings > Cellular on your iPhone.
❖ Select a line (located below SIMs) if the device has two SIMs.
❖ Take one of the following actions:
   ✓ To make and take calls on your iPad and other devices, click Calls on Additional Devices, choose Allow Calls on other Devices, and then select your iPad
   This enables calls to be placed and received on your iPad alongside additional devices that are signed up using the same Apple ID when they are near your iPhone and linked to Wi-Fi.
   ✓ Toggle on Add Wi-Fi Speaking For Other Devices after tapping Wi-Fi Calling.
   This lets you make and take calls on your iPad along with other devices that are signed in with the same Apple ID password even if your iPhone isn't close by.
❖ Turn on FaceTime & Calls from your iPhone by navigating to Settings> FaceTime on your iPad. Turn on WiFi Calling if prompted.
   ✓ Call someone by tapping on a phone number in Safari, Contacts, the Calendar app, FaceTime, Messages, or Search. Alternatively, launch FaceTime, and choose the FaceTime Sound☏ button after entering a contact/phone number.

✓ When a call comes in, swipe or press the notice to accept it or decline it.

Note: Regardless of whether location services are enabled or not, urgent calls may be placed via Wi-Fi calling and your device's location data can be used for urgent calls to support response operations. Certain carriers could utilize the address you provided while registering for WiFi calling where you are.

USING YOUR IPAD, MAKE AND TAKE PHONE CALLS

❖ Call someone by tapping or clicking on a phone number in Safari, Contacts, Calendar app, FaceTime, Messages, or Search. Alternatively, launch FaceTime, and choose the FaceTime Audio button after entering a contact/phone number.

When you make a call using your iPad using Dual SIM and relay it from another device, the default voice line is used.

❖ When a call comes in, you may choose to answer it or not by swiping, tapping, or clicking the alert.

TRANSFER TASKS FROM YOUR IPAD TO YOUR OTHER DEVICES

You may pick up where you left off on a single gadget (iPhone, iPad, iPad touch, the Mac, or the Apple Watch) and continue on another device using Handoff. You might, for instance, begin responding to an email on the iPad and complete it in Mail on the computer.

Numerous Apple programs, including Calendar, Contacts, and Safari, are compatible with Handoff. Apps from third parties may also function with Handoff.

BEFORE STARTING

When transferring work from an iPad to another device, be careful to do the following:

❖ On both devices, your Apple ID is used TO log in.
❖ You have enabled Bluetooth®, Wi-Fi, and Handoff on your Mac.
❖ You have enabled Wi-Fi, Bluetooth, & Handoff on your iPad as well as another iPhone or iPad.
❖ The Bluetooth range between your devices is around 33 feet / 10 meters.
❖ The bare minimum of iOS 10, iPadOS 13, Mac 10.10, watchOS 1.0, or later, is loaded on each device.

SWITCH TO YOUR IPAD FROM ANOTHER DEVICE

❖ To access the Dock, slide upward from the bottom of any app and pause it.
❖ To continue using the iPad app, hit the Handoff icon located on the right side of the Dock.

SWITCH FROM THE IPAD TO ANOTHER GADGET

To continue using the app on the other gadget, click or press the Handoff symbol.

The iPad app you're using's Handoff icon may be found in the following places on other devices:

❖ Mac: Depending on the Dock's location, at the bottom of its right end.
❖ At the bottom of the Application Switcher screen on an iPhone or iPod touch.
❖ iPad: The Dock's rightmost portion.

DISABLE HANDOFF ON THE DEVICES YOU USE

❖ Navigate to Settings > Settings > AirPlay and Handoff on your iPad, iPhone, or iPod touch.
❖ macOS 13: Select System Preferences from the Apple menu, then select General in the sidebar. Select AirDrop & Handoff from the options on the right. Finally, disable Allow Handoff for this Mac and any iCloud devices.
❖ For macOS 12.5 or lower: Go to System Preferences from the Apple menu, choose General, and then uncheck the box next to "Allow Handoff across this Mac & your iCloud devices."

TRANSFERRING FILES AND IMAGES BETWEEN IPAD & OTHER DEVICES

Using the Universal Clipboard, you may cut or copy information from your iPad—such as a text or picture block—and then paste it to another iPad, iPod touch, iPhone, Mac computer, or iPad.

Note: See Move & copy objects using drag and drop in iPads for details on transferring items inside applications or copying items across apps only on the iPad. See Select, cut, replicate, and paste content on iPad for more on manipulating text on your iPad exclusively inside or between applications.

BEFORE STARTING

Make careful of the following before cutting or copying and pasting between an iPad and another device:

* ❖ On both devices, your Apple ID is used to log in.
* ❖ You have enabled Bluetooth®, Wi-Fi, and Handoff on your Mac.
* ❖ You have enabled Wi-Fi, Bluetooth, & Handoff on your iPad as well as another iPhone or iPad.
* ❖ The Bluetooth range between your devices is around 33 feet and 10 meters.
* ❖ The very minimum of the necessary software is installed on each device: iOS 10, iPadOS 13, macOS 10.12, or above.

CUT, COPY, AND PASTE

* ❖ Copy: Using three fingers, pinch closed.
* ❖ Cut: Twice pinch closed using three fingers.
* ❖ Paste: Use three fingers to pinch open.

Moreover, you may hold and touch a selection before selecting Cut, Copy, and Paste.

Important: You have limited time to cut, copy, & paste your text.

UTILIZE IPAD AIRDROP TO DELIVER OBJECTS TO ADJACENT DEVICES

You may wirelessly share your images, movies, webpages, locations, and more with Mac laptops and other nearby devices via AirDrop.

Both Bluetooth® and Wi-Fi are required for AirDrop to function, therefore both must be switched on. Transfers are protected by encryption for security, and using AirDrop requires that you be logged in with an Apple ID.

As each transfer comes in, the receiver has the option to accept or reject it. There can be cellular fees.

SEND SOMETHING VIA AIRDROP

❖ Once the item is open on your iPad, touch the More option • • • button, AirDrop, Share ⬆, or any other button that brings up the app's sharing choices.

❖ After selecting the AirDrop user you'd like to share with, press the AirDrop icon ⊚. (You may distribute files across your own devices by using AirDrop as well.)

Ask the individual to open the Control Centre and permit AirDrop to accept stuff if they are not seen as a near AirDrop user on your iPad. To transmit to a Mac user, request that they enable AirDrop to find them in the Finder.

Passwords for websites and apps may also be safely shared via AirDrop with an iPhone, iPad, or Mac user. View Passwords and passkeys safely shared over AirDrop on the iPad.

ALLOW ANYONE TO USE AIRDROP TO TRANSFER OBJECTS TO YOUR IPAD

❖ To access the Control Centre, go to the top-left control group, touch and hold it, and then press the AirDrop icon.

❖ To choose the recipients of things, click Contacts Only/Everyone for 10 Minutes.

USE ICLOUD TO AUTOMATICALLY UPDATE YOUR FILES ON YOUR PC AND IPAD.

To access and maintain file sync across all of your devices, you may save a variety of media on iCloud, including photographs, videos, and files. Any modifications you made to a document on one iCloud-connected device are reflected on all connected devices.

If your web browser is compatible, you may use iCloud to access your data from any location. Check out iCloud's system requirements.

Important: Windows 7 or OS X 10.10 (or newer) are needed. On your PC, iPad, and any other web browsers you may be using, you need to be logged in with an Apple ID.

CONFIGURE YOUR IPAD FOR ICLOUD

❖ Navigate to Settings -> [your name] on your iPad. Select "Sign in to your [device]" and input your password and Apple ID if you don't see [your name].

❖ To switch on things you wish to retain in iCloud, tap iCloud.

The iCloud setting screen displays a list of compatible applications and functions along with the iCloud storage meter.

To enable your computer to access your files stored in iCloud Drive, for instance, switch on the service.

CONFIGURE ICLOUD ON A MAC

❖ To configure iCloud functions on a Mac, go to the macOS User's Guide and follow the steps.

❖ Activate the same stuff that you did with the iPad.

SWITCH THE IPAD ON OR OFF

To turn the iPad on, press the top button. To switch off your iPad, use the Settings app or the top button (or the volume key on some models).

You may try resetting your iPad by switching it off and back on if it's not functioning as it should. Try getting it to start over if turning it on and off doesn't resolve the problem.

TURN ON OR OFF THE IPAD (FOR VERSIONS WITH THE TOUCH ID OR FACE ID BUTTONS ON TOP)

Try these steps if the Home button is absent on your iPad:

❖ Hold down the top key of the iPad to turn it on till the Apple logo shows.
❖ To turn off your iPad, press and hold both the top and one of the volume buttons at the same time, then move the slider.

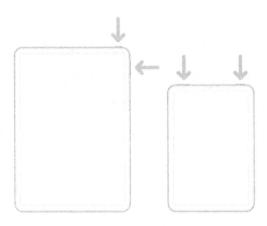

Two distinct iPad versions with their displays pointing up are shown. The top button is located close to the right edge, while the volume upward and downward buttons are located on the right-hand side of the gadget in the leftmost picture. The volume upward and downward keys are located on the device's top, close to the left side, as shown in the figure on the right. It displays the top button close to the right edge.

FLIP THE IPAD (IPAD MODELS WITH THE HOME BUTTON) ON OR OFF

❖ Hold down the top button of the iPad to turn it on till the Apple logo shows.
❖ Click and hold the upper button on the iPad, then move the slider to turn it off.

An example of a model iPad with the home button. It displays the top button close to the right edge

You may adjust the slider under settings > General > Shut Down to switch off any model.

RESTART THE IPAD WITH FORCE

Try forcing the iPad to reset if it isn't responding and you can't get it to restart by turning it off and back on.

IPAD MODELS USING TOUCH ID OR FACE ID IN THE VERY TOP BUTTON THAT NEED A FORCE RESTART

Try these steps if the Home button is absent on your iPad:

❖ The volume button closest to the upper button should be pressed and rapidly released.
❖ The volume icon farthest away from the highest button should be pressed and rapidly released.
❖ Hold down the button on top.
❖ Release the upper button when you see the Apple logo.

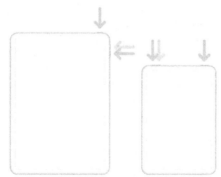

Two distinct iPad versions with their displays pointing up are shown. The device's right-side volume up and down controls are seen in the leftmost figure. It displays the top button close to the right edge. The volume upward and downward keys are located on the device's top, close to the left side, as shown in the figure on the right. It displays the top button close to the right edge.

FOR IPAD DEVICES THAT HAVE A HOME BUTTON, FORCE RESTART

Simultaneously press down on the Home and Top buttons. Release both buttons when you see the Apple logo.

A drawing of an iPad showing the Home button located at the bottom of the tablet. It displays the top button close to the right edge.

IPADOS UPDATE

Your information and settings don't change when you upgrade to the newest version of iPadOS.

Make sure you manually or automatically back up your iPad before updating.

AUTOMATICALLY UPDATE IPAD

Perform the following actions if you didn't enable updates automatically when you initially set up your iPad:

- Select Automatic Updates under Settings > Software > General Update.
- Activate the Automatic Install and Download of the iOS Updates listed below.

The iPad charges and connects to Wi-Fi overnight while downloading and installing any available updates. Before a new version is installed, you are informed.

MANUALLY UPDATE THE IPAD

You may search and then install software updates at any time.

Select Software > General Update under Settings.

The screen displays the iPadOS version that is presently installed along with any available updates.

Navigate to General > Settings > Software Update > Automatically Updated Software to disable automatic updates.

UTILIZING YOUR PC TO UPDATE

- Use a cord to connect your PC and iPad.
- Take any of the following actions:
  - ✓ For Mac users running macOS 10.15 or higher: Choose your iPad from the Finder sidebar, and then select General at the very top of the window.
  - ✓ To access iTunes on your Mac (Mac OS 10.14 or older) or a Windows PC, launch the application, choose the iPad-like button located in the upper

left corner of Apple's iTunes window, and then select Summary.

❖ To check for updates, click Check.

❖ Click Update to install any available updates.

IPAD BACKUP

iPad backups may be made on a PC or via iCloud. See About backup for the iPad, iPhone, and iPod touch to determine which approach is right for you

Advice: You may move your data to a new iPad by using the backup of your old iPad.

ICLOUD BACKUP FOR IPAD

❖ Navigate to Settings > iCloud > Backup in iCloud under [your name].

❖ Activate iCloud Backup.
Your iPad is automatically backed up via iCloud every day when it is powered on, locked, and linked to Wi-Fi.
Note: Depending on your carrier, you may be able to use your cellular network to perform an iPad backup on Wi-Fi + Cellular devices that support 5G. Toggle between turning on and off Backup Over Mobile by going to Settings> [your username] > iCloud > Apple Backup.

❖ Click Back Up Now to manually conduct a backup.

Go to Settings> [your name] > iCloud > Configure Account Storage > Backup to see your iCloud backups. Select the backup from the selection, and finally choose

Turn Off & Delete from iCloud to remove it from the device you're using. Tap Delete to remove a backup that was made utilizing the same Apple ID that was used on a separate device.

Note: An application's data is saved in iCloud if you enable it to utilize iCloud synchronization (in Setting > [your name] > iCloud > Display All). It isn't included in the iCloud backup since it is automatically updated across all of your devices.

USING YOUR MAC, CREATE AN IPAD BACKUP

- ❖ Use a cord to connect your PC and iPad.
- ❖ Choose your iPad from the Finder window on your Mac.
  You must have macOS 10.15 or higher to utilize the Finder for backing up your iPad. Use iTunes to back up your iPad if you're using an older macOS version.
- ❖ Click General in the Finder window's top menu.
- ❖ To backup all of your iPad's data to this Mac, choose that option.
- ❖ Choose "Encrypt local backup" to encrypt the backup data and password-protect it.
- ❖ Click Return Now.

Note: If you configure Wi-Fi syncing, you may also connect your iPad wirelessly to your computer.

MAKE A WINDOWS PC BACKUP OF YOUR IPAD

- ❖ Use a cord to connect your PC and iPad.

- ❖ Tap the iPad button located in the upper left corner of the iTunes screen on your PC.
- ❖ Select Summary.
- ❖ (Below Backups) Click Back Up Now.
- ❖ Choose "Encrypt local backup," provide a password, and then tap Set Password to encrypt your backups.

To see the computer's backups, choose Edit > Options and then Devices. In the backup list, encrypted backups are shown with a lock symbol.

SET THE IPAD BACK TO THE ORIGINAL SETTINGS

Without deleting your material, you may restore settings to their original state.

Make a backup of your iPad's settings before restoring it to its original state if you wish to preserve them. For instance, you may wish to restore your prior settings using a backup if you're attempting to address an issue but changing everything back to its original settings isn't working.

- ❖ Select General > Transfer / Reset iPad > Reset from the Settings menu.
- ❖ Select a choice:
  Warning: All of your material will be erased if you select the Erase All Material and Settings option. Refer to Erase iPad.
- ✓ Reset All Settings: Refer to All configurations that are erased or returned to their original state,

including those related to the network, the keyboard lexicon, location, privacy, and Apple Pay cards. Media and data are not erased.

✓ Reset Network Settings: This eliminates all network configurations. In addition, manually trusted certificates (for websites, for example) are converted to untrusted, and the device name provided in Setting > General > About is changed to "iPad."

You may also disable roaming of your cell data.

Resetting network settings erases all previously used network and VPN configurations that weren't set up using MDM (mobile device management) or configuration profiles. You are disconnected from whatever network you are connected to when Wi-Fi is switched off and then turned back on. Both Ask to Connect to Networks and Wi-Fi are still enabled.

Go to Configurations > General > VPN and Device Management, choose the configuration profile, and then click Erase Profile to erase the VPN settings that were installed by that profile. Other accounts and settings that the profile provides are likewise deleted in this way.

Go to setting > General > VPN and Device Management, choose the management, and then click Delete Management to delete the MDM-installed network settings. Other MDM-provided settings and certificates are also deleted in this way.

✓ Reset Keyboard Dictionary: When you reject words that the iPad proposes you enter, you may add new words to the keypad dictionary. Just the terms you've added are deleted when you reset the keyboard dictionary.

✓ Reset the Homepage Layout: This feature restores the pre-installed applications to the way they appeared on the main screen.

✓ Reset Location and Privacy: This action restores the privacy settings and location services to their initial state.

RESTORE THE WHOLE IPAD'S CONTENTS FROM A BACKUP

To a new or freshly deleted iPad, you may restore information, settings, and applications from a backup.

Important: You need to back up your iPad first.

DATA RESTORATION WITH AN ICLOUD BACKUP

❖ Activate a freshly deleted or new iPad.

❖ Take any of the following actions:

✓ After selecting Recover from iCloud Backup and Set Up Manually, adhere to the on-screen directions.

✓ If you have additional iOS 11–iOS 13–compatible iPhone, iPad, and iPod touch, you may utilize Quick Start to have your new device configured immediately. After bringing the two devices near to one another, securely replicate a large number of one's settings, preferences, as well as iCloud Keychain by following the on-screen directions. After that, you may use your iCloud backup to transfer the remaining data and material to your new smartphone.

Or, you may wirelessly move all of your data from your old device to the new one if both of them have iOS 12.4, iPad operating system 13, or later. Keep all of your gadgets charged and close to one another while the transfer procedure is ongoing.

DATA RESTORATION FROM A PC BACKUP

❖ Connect a brand-new or recently deleted iPad over USB to the backup PC.

❖ Take any of the following actions:
  ✓ Using macOS 10.15 or afterward a Mac: Choose your iPad from the Finder sidebar, pick Trust, and then choose "Restore from this backup."
  ✓ On a Windows computer or a Mac running macOS 10.14 or earlier: Launch the iTunes application, choose Summary, click Restore Backup, and then click the iPad-shaped icon in the upper left corner of the iTunes window.

❖ Select the backup file from the list and press the Proceed button.

To restore your information and settings, you must first input the password if the backup is encrypted.

CHAPTER EIGHT

THE CAMERA APP

USE THE IPAD CAMERA TO SNAP PICTURES

Discover how to use your iPad's Camera  to capture amazing pictures. Select from a variety of camera settings, including Photo, Pano, & Square, and take advantage of features like Live and Burst photos.

Say something like "Open Camera," Siri. Acquire proficiency with Siri.

In the photo mode, the camera opens.

CAPTURE A PICTURE

When you launch Camera, the default mode that appears is called Photo. To capture still images, use the Photo mode. To choose between a different mode, like

Video, Pano, time-lapse, Slo-mo, or portrait (on compatible models), swipe the mode selection up or down.

❖ To access Camera in Photo mode, flick left on the locked screen or tap Camera 📷 on the main screen.
❖ To snap a picture, hit any of the volume buttons or the shutter button.

On devices that feature True Tone Flash, hit the Flash button and choose Auto, On, / Off to switch the flash either on or off.

Stabilize the device and compose your photo before starting the timer. Select 3 or 10 seconds by tapping the Timer button.

Note: When the camera is in operation, a green dot shows at the very top of the display for your protection. Refer to Manage Hardware feature access.

ENLARGE OR REDUCE IN SIZE

❖ To zoom in or out on any model, launch the Camera app and pinch the screen.
❖ Based on your model, choose one of the following actions:
  ✓ On the left edge of the screen, tap 1x.
  ✓ Move the slider to the left or right on the screen.
  ✓ Drag the slider to the left or right after touching and holding the zoom settings on the left-hand side of the screen.

CAPTURE A PANORAMIC IMAGE

❖ After selecting Pano mode, press the Shutter button.
❖ Maintaining the arrow's center line, pan gently in its direction.

Panorama mode on the camera. The path of the pan is indicated with an arrow that points right from the center.

❖ Finally, press the Shutter button once again.
To pan into the other way, tap the arrow. Turn the iPad to landscape mode to pan vertically. A vertical pan also can be reversed in direction.

TAKE ACTION PHOTOS BY USING THE BURST MODE

Burst mode captures several fast-moving images so you have a variety to choose from. Both the front and back cameras may be used to capture burst images.

❖ Select the Square or Photo mode.
❖ Hold down the shutter key to snap quick pictures.

How many shots you took is shown on the counter.

❖ To stop, raise your finger.
❖ Press the Burst thumbnails, then press Select to pick the pictures you want to save.

The recommended pictures to save are shown by grey dots under the thumbnails.
❖ To save a specific picture, hit the circle on the bottom-right area of each one, then choose Done.

Tap the thumbnail and then the Delete option 🗑 to remove the full collection of Burst photographs.

TAKING A LIVE PICTURE

A live snapshot records everything that occurs, including sound, just before and after you've taken the picture.

❖ Select Photo mode on devices that allow Live Photos.
❖ To turn live pictures on (yellow is on), tap the Live Picture button ◎.
❖ To snap a picture, use the Shutter button.

Live photos in your albums have the word "Live" in the upper-left corner. Editing Live Photos allows you to apply effects like Loop and Bounce.

SNAPPING A SELF PICTURE

Utilize the Camera app on your iPad to snap a selfie in picture mode.

SNAP A SELFIE

❖ Open Camera

- ❖ Tap your Camera Chooser Back-Facing key 🔄 or, depending on your model, the Camera Chooser Back-Facing button 🔄 to switch to the front camera.
- ❖ Align your iPad so that it faces you.
- ❖ To snap a picture, hit any of the volume buttons or the shutter button.

MIRRORED THE PRIMARY CAMERA

Go to Settings > Camera, then choose Mirror Front Camera to snap a mirrored selfie that records the image as it appears in the camera frame.

On devices that enable Retina Flash, choose Auto, On, / Off after tapping the Flash button ⚡ to toggle the flash either on or off.

Tip: To expand your range of vision and zoom out, hit the left-hand Zoomed In button 🔄, depending on the model. To zoom back in, use the Zoom Out button 🔄.

USE THE IPAD CAMERA TO TAKE A PORTRAIT SELFIE

On compatible devices, the Camera allows you to add a depth-of-field effect to your selfies. This effect produces a gorgeously blurred backdrop while maintaining facial definition. You may also adjust the amount of background blur and the Portrait Lights effect based on the model of your iPad.

TAKE A PORTRAIT-STYLE SELFIE

❖ Click Camera, then choose the Portrait setting.
❖ Place the device in front of you and use the portrait box to frame your image.
❖ To snap a picture, use the Shutter button.

USE THE IPAD CAMERA TO RECORD VIDEOS

To capture slow-motion and time-lapse films on your iPad, switch between modes in the Camera app.

RECORDING A VIDEO

❖ Select the Video mode.
❖ To begin recording, hit one of the two-volume buttons or tap the Record button. You have the following options when recording:
   ✓ The screen may be pinch-to-zoom in and out.
   ✓ Be sure to touch 1x, then use the slider (on compatible devices) to zoom in more accurately.
❖ To end the recording, hit one of the two-volume buttons or tap the Record button.
   Note: When the camera is in operation, a green dot shows at the top of the screen for your protection. Refer to Manage Hardware feature access.

CAPTURE 4K OR HD VIDEO

You may capture video using high-quality formats such as HD, 4K, HD (PAL), & 4K (PAL) depending on the type of your iPad.

Note: Larger video files are produced by greater resolutions and faster frame rates.

- ❖ Navigate to Settings > Camera > Video Recording.
- ❖ Choose from a list of supported video formats & frame rates on your iPad.

Note: A lot of nations and areas in Europe, Asia, Africa, & South America utilize the PAL television visual format.

TO ADJUST THE VIDEO'S FRAME RATE AND RESOLUTION, USE THE QUICK TOGGLES.

When your iPad is in video mode, you may adjust the frame rates and video resolution by using the quick switches at the very top of the screen. Go to Settings > Camera > Video Recording, and activate Video Format Control to see the fast toggles.

MAKE A VIDEO IN SLOW MOTION

When you shoot a video in slow motion, it starts normally but when we play it back, it seems to be moving slowly. Additionally, you may modify your movie to have the slow-motion action begin and end at a predetermined period.

- ❖ Select the Slo-mo mode.
- ❖ To begin and end the recording, hit the Record icon or the appropriate volume button.
  Click the video thumbnails, then choose Edit to have some of the movie play at a slower pace and the remainder play at standard speed. To choose the portion you want to replay in slow motion, slide the bars that are vertical underneath the frame viewer.

You may adjust the resolution and frame rate based on your model. The final video file is bigger the higher the quality and the quicker the frame rate.

Navigate to parameters > Camera > Recording Slo-mo to adjust the slow-motion recording parameters.

RECORD A TIME-LAPSE FILM

❖ Select the Time-lapse setting.
❖ Place your iPad in a position where you wish to record a sunset, moving traffic, or other event over time.
❖ To begin recording, hit the Record button; to end recording, tap it once again.

MODIFY THE AUTO FPS PARAMETERS

When there is poor light, iPad models that feature Auto FPS may automatically lower the frame rate to 24 frames per second.

Select Settings ⚙ > Camera > Video Recording, and then do any of the below actions:

❖ Activate Auto Low Light FPS on the iPad (9th version), iPad Pro 11-square inch (1st and 2nd generations), & iPad Pro 12.9-square inch (3rd and 4th gcnerations).
❖ Regarding the iPad Pro 11-inch (3rd version and later), iPad Pro 12.9-inch (5th version and later), iPad Air (4th version & earlier), iPad mini (6th version), and iPad Pro 10th generation: Select Auto

FPS and apply it to either 30- or 60-frame-per-second videos.

SECURE THE WHITE BALANCE CONFIGURATION

When filming movies on your iPad, you can disable the white balance to enhance precise color capture depending on the illumination.

Select Record Video under Settings ⚙ > Camera, and then activate Lock White Balance.

ADJUST THE ADVANCED CAMERA SETTINGS

Discover how to manually modify the focus or exposure, activate and deactivate the shutter volume, and alter other iPad camera settings.

MODIFY THE EXPOSURE AND FOCUS

The iPad camera automatically adjusts focus and exposure before shooting a picture. It also uses face identification to evenly distribute exposure across a variety of faces. To manually modify the exposure and focus, use the following actions:

❖ To see the autofocus region and exposure level, tap the screen.
❖ To shift the focus area, tap the desired location.
❖ To change the exposure, drag the Adjust Brightness icon up or down close to the focus area.
Press and hold the focusing area until you see the AE/AF Lock; click the screen to unlock the settings.

This locks your manual focus & exposure settings for forthcoming pictures.

HOW TO MAKE YOUR SHOT STRAIGHT BY USE A GRID

Go to Settings ⚙ > Camera, then choose Grid to enable a grid that will help you align and arrange your photo on the camera screen.

Once you've taken a picture, you may utilize the Photos app's editing features to further align images and change their vertical and horizontal perspective. See Straighten and modify your viewpoint.

PRESERVING THE CAMERA'S SETTINGS

To prevent it from being reset when you open the Camera again, you may preserve the last photo mode you used.

❖ Navigate to Preserve Settings under Settings ⚙ > Camera.
❖ Additionally, you may save Live Photos settings on compatible models.

ADJUSTING THE SHUTTER VOLUME

Using the volume button on the side of your iPad, you may change the camera shutter sound's loudness. Alternatively, activate Control Centre by swiping down from the top-right side of the screen, then move the volume slider 🔊.

Note: When the Live Pictures button ⊚ is used, there is no sound from the shutter.

Hold down the button that controls the volume to muffle the shutter sound. If your iPad includes a Ring/Silent switch, you may also utilize it.

Note: It is not possible to muffle the shutter sound in certain nations or areas.

SWITCH THE SCENE DETECTION ON AND OFF

When you use the Scene Detection option, your camera may recognize what you're shooting and apply a customized style that highlights the best aspects of the scene.

By default, Scene Detection is enabled. Go to Settings > Camera, choose Scene Detection, and then click the "Off" button.

iPad Pro 12.9-inch (5th version & later), iPad Pro 11-square inch (3rd version and later), iPad Air (4th version & later), and iPad mini (6th version) are all compatible with Scene Detection.

SWITCH ON AND OFF LENS CORRECTION

For more realistic-looking images, the Lens Correction option modifies pictures produced with the front or Ultra Wide camera.

By default, Lens Correction is enabled. Go to Settings ⚙ > Camera, choose Lens Correction, and then click the Off button.

iPad mini (6th version), iPad Air (5th version), iPad Pro 12.9-square inch (5th version & later), iPad Pro 11-square inch (3rd Generation and later), & iPad (9th Generation and after) are all compatible with Lens Correction.

USING AN IPAD, VIEW, SHARE, & PRINT IMAGES

Your camera's captured images and movies are all stored in Photos. Enable iCloud Photos on all of your devices (i.e., those running iOS 8.1, iPad operating system 13, or newer) to automatically upload and make all new images and videos accessible in Photos.

Note: Videos and pictures are tagged with location information that applications and photo-sharing websites may access if Location Services is enabled under Settings ⚙ > Security and Privacy > Location Services.

LOOK AT YOUR PICTURES

❖ Select the picture thumbnail located under the Shutter button in Camera.
❖ To see the latest pictures you've shot, swipe right. To reveal or conceal the controls, tap the screen.
❖ To see all of your stored images and movies, tap All Photos.

SHARE & PRINT YOUR IMAGES

❖ When looking at a picture, click the Share icon. ⬆

❖ Choose an option like AirDrop, Mail, and Messages to share your picture.

❖ Swipe up to choose Print from the list of options to print your picture.

UPLOAD IMAGES AND KEEP THEM CURRENT ON ALL DEVICES

Upload images and videos from the device to iCloud using iCloud Photos, then use the same Apple ID to view the files on other devices. When you want to preserve space on the device or maintain your picture collection current across various devices, iCloud Photos might be helpful. Navigate to Settings ⚙ > Photos to enable iCloud Photos.

USE THE IPAD CAMERA TO SCAN A QR CODE

QR (Quick Response) codes may be scanned with the Camera or the Code Scan to find connections to websites, applications, tickets, discounts, and more. A QR code is instantly recognized by the camera and highlighted.

READING A QR CODE WITH THE CAMERA

❖ After turning on the camera, place the iPad such that the code shows on the screen.

❖ To access the relevant webpage or app, tap the notice that shows up on the screen.

FROM CONTROL CENTRE, LAUNCH THE CODE SCANNER

❖ Navigate to Settings 🎛️ > Control Centre and choose Code Scanner by tapping the Insert button ➕.

❖ To see the code on the screen, position the iPad after opening the Control Centre, and tapping the Code Scanner.

❖ Click the flashlight's button to turn it on and add extra light.

Made in the USA
Coppell, TX
30 November 2024

41406724R00134